THE *Original*

CHRISTMAS CAROL

STEPHEN DAVEY

The Original Christmas Carol

Author: Stephen Davey
Editor: Jarl K. Waggoner
Body Layout: Kristin Preston
Photo of Stephen: Sam Gray Portraits, Raleigh, NC (samgrayportraits. com)
ISBN

Published by Charity House Publishers

Charity House Publishers, Inc.
2703 Jones Franklin Road
Suite 105
Cary, NC 27518
USA

www.wisdomonline.org

Table of Contents

Foreward 7

1. Surprises in the Family Tree 9

2. Gems from the Genealogy 23

3. The Song of Mary 37

4. The Surrender of Bliss 49

5. From Riches to Rags 63

6. The Announcement 75

7. The Presentation of the Lamb 87

8. The King-Makers 103

9. Israel's Most Wanted 119

10. More Than the Legend of Zeus 133

Endnotes 147

Foreword

In 1843 Charles Dickens wrote and published A Christmas Carol. His novella, originally entitled A Christmas Carol in Prose, Being a Ghost-Story of Christmas, was enthusiastically received and has since become a Christmas tradition in its own right. Interestingly, though its title would suggest a song, the story is written in prose, as the original title indicates. Yet one does not have to stretch the language too much to see that like the Christmas carols we sing each year, Dickens' book is an uplifting story of redemption and joy—a memorable story that has been read and shared from one generation to the next, reminding us that there is hope for even the most wicked of people, and that hope rests in the coming of Jesus Christ into the world.

Like a joyous song, the Bible reveals that God the Son, Jesus Christ, entered our world as a man over two thousand years ago. It is a story of redemption set in history and declared in the prose of the New Testament, as well as in the songs of Mary, Elizabeth, and the angels who announced Jesus' birth. In this book, Stephen Davey draws upon his years of preaching the Bible to present the original Christmas carol—the grand, biblical revelation of the birth of our Savior.

From Matthew's genealogy of Christ, which sets His coming in human history, to the dramatic intervention in Mary's life, which set her and Joseph on a unique course, to the announcement to the world and the testimony of witnesses drawn from the lowest and highest of society, the Christmas story comes alive in these ten chapters. And like a Christmas carol filling the winter night with chords of joy, they remind us that the One born in such humble circumstances so long ago is the God-man who came to this earth so that we might inherit the riches of heaven.

This story is a glorious and joyous song that bears repeating over and over, year after year. I invite you to join the chorus as Stephen Davey unveils the Bible's Original Christmas Carol.

–Jarl K. Waggoner

Chapter 1

Surprises in the Family Tree
Matthew 1:1-17

Tracing one's genealogy is all the rage today. I have read that more than 100 million people a year do some type of research online in relation to their family tree. And the number is rising.

But as Sue Shellenbarger explains, "Researching your ancestry doesn't always turn up heroes and royalty. It may turn up a felon, a bigamist or another unsavory character."[1]

> New York filmmaker Heather Quinlan found more than a few skeletons when digging into her ancestors' closet. Among them: Thomas Fagan, her grandmother's great-grandfather, who had killed a man during a drunken bar fight in 1868 (reportedly hitting him over the head with a chair in self-defense).[2]

Quinlan also discovered that a murderous feud had taken the lives of family members back in the 1830s. One ancestor who killed a relative was caught and hanged. Her great-great-great-grandfather was also caught and jailed but escaped after the jailer forgot to lock his cell door.[3]

Sometimes the skeletons found in the family tree are much closer to where you are.

"Ron Arons set out to piece together his family's past after discovering a box of documents and a family tree following his parents' death." He had been raised believing his forefathers were all upstanding citizens in their community, but his research actually revealed that his great-grandfather was married to two women at the same time. He was arrested after a rather wild police chase and served time in Sing Sing prison for bigamy.[4]

Genealogist Crista Cowan had a client who discovered, to his horror, that his great-great-grandfather was the infamous "sausage king" of Chicago. While this man was the owner of a meatpacking plant, he had earned his nickname only because he had murdered his wife and disposed of her body in a sausage grinder.[5] Imagine discovering that kind of family secret!

Shellenbarger also recounts the story of another family researcher, Jean Wilcox Hibben, who discovered the real story behind a rather proud family legend. She set out to explore the story she had often heard as a child about a great-grandfather who had served heroically alongside General William Sherman during Sherman's historic march to the sea and the capture of Savannah, Georgia, during the Civil War.

Instead of finding commendations of her great-grandfather's bravery, she learned that he never saw any action at all; in fact, he was discharged after only a few months for complaining about his poor health due to "excessive marching and falling over a log." He was not exactly the family hero after all. When Hibben broke the news to her family, it was not well-received.[6]

There are times when you'd rather not know who's hanging from your family tree!

Of course, there are times when you might find something of which to be proud—but even then, you need to be careful.

One person wrote, "One day I sat down with my daughter and explained with great pride that her grandfather was a preacher, her great-great-grandfather was a preacher, and her great-great-great grandfather was a preacher. To which she replied, "Wow! We sure come from a long line of *grandfathers*."[7]

The most famous family tree in existence—one that has been researched and studied for centuries—happens to be found on the first page of the New Testament. It's been inspected more than any other genealogy in human history, because if this family tree isn't correct, not one of us is going to heaven. If this genealogy is not true and accurate, Christianity would be proven to be just another empty religion with a truckload of empty promises.

Before the carol of Christmas can be sung, the Christ of Christmas must be certified.

WHAT JESUS' GENEALOGY CLAIMS

The record of the genealogy of Jesus the Messiah . . . (Matthew 1:1a)

The book of Matthew begins with these words: **The record of the genealogy of Jesus. Record** is the Greek *biblos*, meaning "book." **Genealogy** is the Greek word *genesis*. This, then, is the book of the genesis of Jesus—the beginning, the roots, the generations, of Jesus.

This phrase isn't found anywhere else in the New Testament. However, the exact same phrase appears in the Greek translation of the Old Testament in Genesis 5:1, which the New American Standard Bible translates, "This is the book of the generations of Adam."

Adam's book represents the human race, and everyone related to Adam has one thing in common. The apostle Paul writes, "In Adam all die" (1 Corinthians 15:22).

However, in 1 Corinthians 15:45, Paul refers to Jesus as "the last Adam." In other words, Jesus is the head of a new race.

You become a descendant of Adam by being born into the human race. You become a descendant of Jesus Christ by being born again into the redeemed race.

The book of Adam is a book of obituaries. Genesis 5 is a long funeral march. Over and over again, you read, "and he died . . . and he died . . . and he died."

The book of Jesus is a book of life. Paul refers to believers having their names in the "book of life" (Philippians 4:3), and John the apostle similarly refers to the Lamb's "book of life" (Revelation 13:8).

If you are related to Jesus by faith and trust in Him, you've been given the right and privilege to become children of God (John 1:12). So even though you die because you are related by birth to Adam, you'll live forever in heaven because you are related by faith to Jesus.

Jesus said, "I am the resurrection and the life; he who believes in Me will live even if he dies" (John 11:25).

The genealogy of Jesus is a genealogy you can join; it's a family tree you can climb into, by faith in the Messiah, Jesus. While the genealogy in Matthew 1 lists Jesus' biological ancestors, it also points to His spiritual family, those written in the Book of Life. We see this in the claim it makes. Matthew says this is **the record of the genealogy of Jesus**, but who is Jesus? He is the **Messiah**. *Christ* is the Greek equivalent of the Hebrew Messiah. Both mean "Anointed One."

Jesus is the Messiah! This was a bold claim but one the Jewish people had heard before, many times over.

A dozen or more people had already made that claim, and even more would make messianic claims after Jesus' resurrection and ascension.

Around AD 44, a man named Theudas apparently made messianic claims. Josephus, the first-century Jewish historian, reported that Theudas claimed to be a prophet and many were deluded by his claims and followed him. He promised his followers that if they went out with him to the Jordan River, he would part the waters as their new deliverer. The Roman army caught up to the group, however, and killed many of them, including Theudas, whose head they severed and prominently displayed back in Jerusalem to discourage any other followers.[8]

A tradition has lingered that Simon the Magician, introduced in Acts 8, eventually gathered a following around his claim to be the Messiah. Legend has it that he promised his followers he would fly through the air but he died in the attempt.

According to the book of Revelation, at the end of human history, another man is going to step forward and amass a global following. That man also will claim to be the Messiah. He is better known to us as the Antichrist.

While Jews might dismiss these opening words of Matthew as presenting just another messianic pretender, the combination of terms in the rest of the verse would make every Jewish leader leap from his chair and rush to the Sanhedrin, where the genealogical records were kept secure, to check out this amazing claim. That's because Matthew not only made the claim that Jesus is the Messiah, but he also provided the genealogical support for that claim.

WHAT JESUS' GENEALOGY ACCOMPLISHES

It Validates the Royalty of Jesus Christ

. . . the son of David, the son of Abraham. (Matthew 1:1b)

Jesus, Matthew declared, is **the son of David, the son of Abraham**.

Now clearly Matthew knew Abraham came before David, but here he reverses the order to get everybody's undivided attention. Here is the opening, and rather surprising, reality: Jesus is royalty—He's from the direct line of King David.

We might paraphrase this opening line of Jesus' genealogy as an announcement from Matthew: "Hey, Israel here is the King! Jesus, the Messiah is the legal heir to the throne of David. Go ahead. Inspect the records; evaluate the evidence of His lineage. Then read His biography."

I agree with evangelical authors who point out that to this very day, the Jewish people will argue against the resurrection of Jesus but not against the *genealogy* of Jesus.

The Jewish leaders checked it out, line by line, and found it to be true. Jesus was indeed a legal heir as a direct descendant of David.

In fact, Jesus is a descendant of a dozen more kings, all listed in this genealogy.

Jewish leaders knew **the son of David**, the true king, would bring healing to their land and to the people of Israel. In Matthew's Gospel, Jesus is called *Son of David* nine different times.

Tolkien, in his massive parable entitled *The Lord of the Rings*, put the messianic promise this way: "The hands of the king are the hands of the healer."[9]

Jesus offered Israel both a King and a Healer in a very literal way. He was unmistakably related to royalty, and He was undeniably a divine healer.

The connection between *who He was* as the Son of David and *what He did* as the Son of God was clear. That's why early in His ministry, two blind men followed Jesus, calling out, "Have mercy on us, Son of David!" (Matthew 9:27).

Even when Jesus traveled to neighboring regions, the people expected Him to exercise His royal claim through the power of healing. Two other blind men were sitting by the roadside outside Jericho, and when they heard Jesus was going by, they shouted, "Lord, have mercy on us, Son of David" (Matthew 20:30).

Matthew is essentially saying at the very outset of Jesus' biography—and then throughout the rest of his Gospel account—"Check out the evidence in His ancestry. He is royalty. This unimpressive peasant Boy, born in squalor and obscurity, the adopted Son of a carpenter, is, in fact, in the direct line of kings. And look, there is healing in His hands."

It Proves the Faithfulness of God

God promised that in Abraham all the world would be blessed (Genesis 12:3; 22:18). Ultimately, this meant the Messiah would be a member of the Jewish race, which came from Abraham, through Isaac and Jacob.

Later, God promised David that the Messiah would come through His family.

Tucked into God's promise to David was something David didn't fully understand: a future-tense application of the prophetic promise we believers will one day see come to pass. God said to David, "I will raise up your descendant after you, who will come forth from you, and I will establish . . . the throne of his kingdom forever" (2 Samuel 7:12-13).

That kingdom is yet to come.

In showing that Jesus is the Son of David and the Son of Abraham, Matthew is showing us that God keeps His word. He is faithful to His promise.

And by the way, when God promised Abraham a descendant who would be a blessing to the world, Abraham probably thought the son God was referring to would be Isaac. In the fullest sense, however, the ultimate fulfillment of that promise from God to Abraham wouldn't arrive until forty-two generations later.[10]

If you thought God was taking a long time to answer you and fulfill a promise He made to you, can you hold on a little longer?

It Reveals the Sovereignty of God

This genealogy is carefully structured by Matthew. The names listed were intentionally selected under the guidance of the Holy Spirit.

Some names are left out, so that there are three sections of fourteen names each, assuming Matthew intended Jeconiah to be counted twice. Many believe this structure was designed to aid in memorizing the list.

But while Matthew has arranged the names on paper, God had arranged them in history. Paul connects the dots when he writes to the Galatians, "But when the fullness of the time came, God sent forth His Son" (Galatians 4:4).

At the *perfect time*, God sent forth His Son!

God designed all of human history around the birth of His Son. That makes what we call Christmas the very center of history.[11]

But still, the timing of God might seem a bit early to some of us. Doug O'Donnell wrote with humor and realism, asking why God didn't send His Son to be born and minister, to die and rise again in the twenty-first century instead of the first century.

> Why didn't he come to earth during the era of television, video, and the Internet, when nearly all that he said and did could be precisely documented? Can't you just picture CNN reporters

and paparazzi camped a few feet away from Jesus and the Twelve for three years straight. Can't you imagine a streaming video of his each and every movement? Can't you imagine the ten o'clock news starting every night with something from the life of Christ?—"Today Jesus healed ten lepers. We interviewed nine of them. One refused an interview in order to return to Jesus for a word of thanks."[12]

And can you imagine the cameras catching the resurrection on film? Wouldn't that have been much better? Not really. To wish for that is to wish for God to remove from our faith the need for *faith*.

Even with all the eyewitness accounts of the Lord's miraculous work in the first century and the firsthand testimony of those who were not only healed but even brought back to life, the Romans were uninterested in Him and the Jews were ultimately infuriated by Him. He was messing up their world. He was disrupting the status quo.

God has provided ample evidence. According to His plan, at just the right time, He sent His son; and by faith we believe the record of evidence He has set before us.

It Highlights the Humility of Jesus

The record of the genealogy of Jesus the Messiah, the son of David, the son of Abraham—these words inform us at the very outset of this Gospel account, that it is the record of a real man, the God-man.

But look at who Jesus is related to in this genealogy. There is Solomon, who, like Ron Aron's great-grandfather, was married to more than one woman. There's David, who sought the Lord but also was as guilty of murder as the sausage king of Chicago.

We find here Abraham, who, although he was a man of faith, also acted as a coward and a liar.

Judah, who is mentioned in verse 2, carried the promise of the royal scepter; however, he hired a woman he thought was a prostitute but ended up being his own daughter-in-law, **Tamar**. She conceived by him and had twins, one of whom carried on the messianic line.

And we also might mention that Judah, along with his brothers, was guilty of selling his little brother, Joseph, to some slave traders heading toward Egypt.

Jesus descended from a line of kings, fifteen of whom are listed by name in this genealogy. They are split between men who followed after God—rather imperfectly, like you and me—and those like **Rehoboam** (verse 7) and **Manasseh** (verse 10), who were fully committed to giving their lives to evil.

Here's Manasseh's bio statement from 2 Kings 21:

- He did more evil than the pagan nations surrounding Judah; he sacrificed his son in the fiery belly of the idol Molech.

- He practiced witchcraft and used divination.

- He had mediums and spiritists in his counsel.

- He placed an idol in the temple precinct.

- He murdered so many people that he filled Jeru-salem from one end to the other with innocent blood.

Jesus is also related to **Jehoshaphat** (Matthew 1:8), a good king who in "his growing fascination with Ahab and Jezebel, went so far as to sanction the marriage of his son Jehoram to their evil daughter Athaliah."[13]

Behind the scenes, Satan was at work trying to pervert and, in fact, stamp out the Davidic line of kings through whom God had promised the Messiah would come.

"No doubt Satan thought he had triumphed . . . [because] after the death of Jehoram, Athaliah massacred every possible claimant to the throne on whom she could lay her hands. She almost succeeded in wiping out the royal line—almost."[14] In God's providence, however, a grandson from the line of David was secretly hidden away for six years and then brought forward to reign.

But here's a point often missed. We're not just talking about wicked family secrets and evil men and women; we're talking about the relatives of Jesus! Sitting in the branches of Jesus' family tree is a collection of really sinful people.

If coming to earth to live as a man weren't humiliating enough for the glorious Son of God, just meet His family: murderers, adulterers, bigamists, polygamists, idol-worshipping, child-sacrificing, immoral, proud men and women.

One author writes, "Jesus comes from the right stock, but it is bad stock."[15] And none of these skeletons are hidden in the closet. They are for everyone to see. Thus, this genealogy highlights the humble, even sordid, background of Jesus the Man.

It also highlights His grace. Jesus didn't come to *praise* His forefathers. He came to *pardon* them.

Paul spelled it out: "It is a trustworthy statement, deserving full acceptance, that Christ Jesus came into the world to save sinners" (1 Timothy 1:15).

He came into the world to save sinners—no one is too sinful to qualify.

And here's more surprising, good news from the family tree of Jesus: If Jesus isn't ashamed of His ancestors, He will not be ashamed of His descendants, all of us redeemed sinners whose names have been written down in the Lamb's Book of Life.

Our names are recorded in the book of Adam's race when we are born. They are recorded in the book of Jesus, the Book of Life, when we put our faith in Christ alone for salvation—when we recognize Him not just as any king but as our King.

Chapter 2

Gems from the Genealogy
Matthew 1:1-17

The Vietnam Veterans Memorial Wall is one of the best-known national monuments in the United States. Located on the National Mall in Washington, DC, this wall is designed with 144 flat panels quarried from black granite. On these granite panels, more than 58,000 names have been engraved and arranged chronologically, according to the day each one died.

There are no lengthy eulogies in sight of the wall. It stands without fanfare and embellishment, bearing silent tribute to 58,318 soldiers who sacrificed their lives for our freedoms.

Among the names listed, 17,000 of them were married; 12 of them were 17 years old and 5 of them were 16; 997 of them were killed on their very first day in the line of fire; and 1,448 of them died on their very last scheduled day of duty.[1]

Carved into that granite wall are volumes of untold stories. The names represent families impacted to this very day.

I found it significant and moving to learn that this stone wall was prepared and polished so that observers can see their own reflection as they read the names—symbolically bringing the past and the present together.

The truth is, every name matters. Every name counts. Every name made a difference in the history of our past and the freedoms we have inherited today.

If you've read through the Bible, you've discovered that God is into names.

Some pages of Scripture are like black granite walls engraved with names—names from the past that have impacted our lives in the present.

Those who read through the entire Bible eventually come to 1 Chronicles, where the first nine chapters consist of one long list of names. It's almost like climbing Mount Everest—you need an oxygen tank to make it through.

But as God reminds us through the apostle Paul in 1 Corinthians 10:11, from His perspective, all these names are significant in more ways than we could ever imagine.

In fact, the wall of Scripture has been prepared and polished so that we see our own reflection in its pages, bringing the significance of the past into the significance of our present and the security of our future.

No list of names is more significant than the one that occupies the opening page of the New Testament book of Matthew. There Matthew connects Jesus to real people, to a real family, to a real Messiah with a real claim to a real throne and a real kingdom.

Myron Augsburger writes in his commentary on this text how he ministered on one occasion in India. There he met a former Hindu who had come to faith in Christ as a young man simply by studying the genealogy of Jesus Christ in Matthew 1. When asked what made this text so profound to him, he stated that for the first time he had found a religion that was actually rooted in history, in contrast to the mythologies of Hinduism and Buddhism.[2]

He had found the real Messiah, rooted in the reality of history. And that's exactly Matthew's purpose in this genealogy.

Let's go back to this inspired wall of names and notice several gems shining with illuminating insight.

GOD'S WAYS ARE OFTEN UNEXPLAINABLE

At the very outset of this genealogy, we are left to wonder why God would choose certain individuals to carry on the royal line. Why, for instance, is **Judah** mentioned in verse 2 instead of Reuben, the firstborn son of Jacob? In fact, Judah had three older brothers. Why did God choose Judah? Was he more deserving than his brothers?

If you dig into the record of Judah's life, you discover that after the ten older sons of Jacob conspired to throw young Joseph into a pit to let him starve to death, Judah came up with the plan to instead sell him to slave traders who were passing by. Judah's plan seemed to be more about making some quick money than showing any kind of mercy.

Reuben, the firstborn son of Jacob, wasn't there when Judah hatched his plan. Reuben had planned to return to the pit later and rescue Joseph, but when he did so, he found his brothers had sold Joseph into slavery. Reuben was the only brother who showed any remorse over what they had done.

Reuben clearly seems the most likely candidate to continue the regal line of the Messiah.

However, many years later, the Bible records in Genesis 44 that these same brothers went to Egypt during a famine in order to buy food for their families. There they unknowingly encountered their brother Joseph, now a powerful leader in Egypt.

After a series of events, Judah was the one who offered his life so that his younger brother Benjamin could be spared. In fact, Judah stepped forward and confessed what they had done years earlier to Joseph. Only then did Joseph reveal his identity to his brothers, and he graciously forgave them (Genesis 45).

So, were Judah's later actions the reason God elevated him above his older brothers? We are not told. God simply doesn't explain why Judah became the head of the royal tribe from which the son of David would descend.

God just did it.

I find it equally surprising that several other men listed in this genealogy, like Judah, are not the firstborn sons in their families.

Isaac and **Jacob** were not firstborn, and King **David** was the youngest brother in his family. **Solomon** was not David's firstborn son. Yet these men were all included in the direct ancestry of Jesus the Messiah.

This goes against the normal inheritance procedures. It upsets tradition. The sovereign plan of God is often unpredictable.

God does what God does, and as believers we cling to the promise that *whatever God does is right* (Daniel 9:14).

- God doesn't explain why He does something in one family and doesn't do it in others.

- God doesn't explain why He allows evil or crime to affect one family member but keeps another family member safe.

- God doesn't explain why one family member suffers hardship or ill health and other family members never do.

The unexplainable nature of God's sovereign plan is seen in this genealogy—and it shows up in yours as well.

God knew who your parents would be; you didn't get to choose them. He planned that they would be healthy and wealthy or ill and poor, or a mixture of both. He planned the country and the century in which you would be born.

He planned every detail and arranged every circumstance so that at the end of your life—and at many times throughout it—you would more deeply worship Him as you trust His unexplainable ways.

As William Cowper wrote in a classic hymn over two centuries ago:

God moves in a mysterious way
His wonders to perform;
He plants His footsteps in the sea
And rides upon the storm.

Deep in unfathomable mines
Of never-failing skill
He treasures up His bright designs
And works His sov'reign will.

Ye fearful saints, fresh courage take;
The clouds ye so much dread
Are big with mercy and shall break
In blessings on your head.[3]

GOD'S PLANS THROUGH HISTORY ARE UNSTOPPABLE

Even though the plan of God involved weak and sinful men and women, His plans for the Redeemer's lineage were unhindered.

Yes, **Tamar** and **Judah** and **Manasseh** and **Bathsheba** and **David** and **Ahaz** are all responsible for their sin, but this genealogy points them, and us, to the cross of the Messiah who died for sinners.

Still, it's obvious that Jesus, though never having sinned Himself, was definitely related to a lot of sinners. What a family He had.

As we've pointed out already, however, if Jesus isn't ashamed to be related to His ancestors, He won't be ashamed to be related to His descendants, you and me, a bunch of sinners brought into the family of God by faith.

Even the sins of the forefathers of Jesus were unable to unhook the railway cars of His lineage from the engine of God's divine purpose.

That's what Satan was attempting to do throughout this historical lineage—disrupt God's plan.

So it is in your life as a follower of Christ. Even though your life is intersected by sin (and you must take it to the cross); even though your life is impacted by other sinners;

and even though your world is governed by Satan, who longs to stop the train of God's will for your life, nothing can derail you from the tracks upon which you will ride one day, secure in Christ, into that heavenly city.

Listen, here's a gem from this genealogy that stretched over thousands of years: you're going to make it home. Because of the unstoppable plan of God, because of your ancestor Jesus, who redeemed you, you're going to arrive one day in heaven.

You might notice the inclusion of the names listed in verses 13-15: **Zerubbabel was the father of Abihud, Abihud the father of Eliakim,** and so on. Nine names follow Zerubbabel in these verses, and we know absolutely nothing about any of them. Nothing.

You can look up every member of the royal family in England and find at least a paragraph on each person.

Matthew chapter 1 reveals the family of the King of Kings! And the only thing we know about the nine men in verses 13-15 is that their lives covered a period of nearly five hundred years of history.[4]

We have no idea what contribution they made; no clue as to whether they were godly or ungodly, followers of Yahweh or idolaters.

For us, time has forgotten why these people mattered. But God hasn't forgotten them, and because they were somehow used by God in the unstoppable chain of events, God's Spirit whispered to Matthew to include these names as well.[5]

To this day the gospel of Christ is advanced by unseen, unknown men and women, young and old, who never make headlines. There are millions of Christians who are making disciples, but we have no idea who most of them are or how they have been woven into the global, unstoppable plan of God. Yet, even though they are unknown to us, they are known to Him.

For all of us, though, this genealogy is a reminder that the same God who guided the unstoppable process of the coming of Christ is guiding the unstoppable progress of the church and of the life of every Christian.[6]

A PERSONAL LINEAGE OF GODLINESS IS UNPREDICTABLE

I just want to touch briefly on this third gem from Jesus' genealogy. It's fascinating to discover in this genealogy that there is no guarantee that a father's godly walk with the Lord will be emulated by his son.

Verse 9 mentions **Hezekiah**, a godly king who cleansed the temple of idols and tore down the high places where idols were worshipped (2 Chronicles 29–31). But Hezekiah's son, **Manasseh**, is described as one of the most wicked kings in the history of the nation. He rebuilt the pagan altars his father had torn down and reinstated idolatry in the Jerusalem temple.

But then, according to 2 Chronicles 33, Manasseh actually repented and began to follow after God. He tore down the idol altars and led the people back into proper temple worship of Yahweh. It is one of the most surprising conversion stories in the Old Testament.

We might naturally think this would change everything for generations.

But then, Manasseh's son, **Amon**, took the throne. He evidently ignored his father's repentance and spent his two-year reign chasing after idols.

And so now we would assume things are going to be messed up for generations.

But then Amon had a son named **Josiah**, who was only eight years old when he ascended the throne. He became one of the nation's godliest reformers. He removed all idol worship from the land and in the process of renovating the temple, he rediscovered the books of Genesis, Exodus, Leviticus, Numbers, and Deuteronomy. This discovery was instrumental in his efforts to lead the nation back to God.[7]

Talk about unpredictability! A godly father has an ungodly son who has an ungodly son who has a godly son.

Here's the point—and this genealogical gem is true in your family tree as well as Jesus'—ultimately, it is the grace of God that is magnified in the conversion of any and every family member. Salvation is not inherited.

Parents, be careful not to take the blame for the unbelief or unfaithfulness of your child. And be especially careful not to take the credit for the belief or faithfulness of your child.

We lay our children at the feet of Jesus and ultimately yield to the plan and the grace and the calling of God.

TESTS OF FAITH AND OBEDIENCE ARE UNFORESEEABLE

This principle is illustrated first in King **Uzziah** (verse 9). Uzziah became king of Judah when he was only sixteen years old, but he followed after God and reigned for fifty-two years.

31

He won great victories as he trusted in God for strength and wisdom. All was well, and the future was bright.

But somewhere the seeds of pride were sown, perhaps in his long string of military victories. Satan patiently baited the hook of self-confidence and pride and then waited . . . and waited . . . and waited some more.

In the account of Uzziah's life, we find this telling and disastrous biographical statement in 2 Chronicles 26:15-16: "His fame spread afar, for he was marvelously helped until he was strong. But when he became strong, his heart was so proud that he acted corruptly, and he was unfaithful to the Lord his God, for he entered the temple of the Lord to burn incense on the altar of incense."

Burning incense on the altar was something only the priests were allowed to do. When Uzziah usurped this role, leprosy broke out on his forehead. He was rushed out of the temple in disgrace, and he ended up quarantined for the remainder of his life. He started so well but ended so poorly.

Faithfulness to God in the past does not guarantee faithfulness to God in the future. And you can believe that Satan has baited a hook for all of us . . . and he is a very patient fisherman.

Don't ever believe the lie that your testimony or your integrity is safely guaranteed. Uzziah started well but ended poorly.

Hezekiah (verse 9) also started well but ended unfaithfully.

We remember Hezekiah offering one of the most unusual prayers God ever answered. When he became ill, the Lord informed him that his illness would lead to his death; but Hezekiah prayed for more time, and God told him that he would live another fifteen years (2 Kings 20:1-6).[8]

Now, you would think after that kind of answered prayer, Hezekiah would never doubt God again. But he did. In fact, later in life, he grew distrustful of God's protection and even though he was warned, he made a secret pact with Babylon, which ultimately became the nation's undoing.

Unforeseen tests of faith and obedience are just around the corner. That is why we must never allow dependence on God to go out of style. His mercy and wisdom and strength are needed new every morning.

THE GAME PLAN OF GOD IS UNCONVENTIONAL

You don't have to read very far in Jesus' genealogy to uncover this fifth gem: God does things differently from anything we would have imagined.

It's as if Matthew rubs the noses of every Jewish reader in the reality of their heritage—which is embarrassing. In verse 3, he mentions **Judah**, who **was the father of Perez and Zerah**, but why would he need to mention their mother, **Tamar**?

As we noted in the last chapter, Tamar was the daughter-in-law of Judah, and she was a widow. She grew impatient in her desire for an heir, so she dressed up like a prostitute and stationed herself where she knew Judah was tending his flocks. She caught his eye, conceived by him, and the sordid story only gets worse.

Why not just omit Tamar from the list? This woman was a Canaanite, which only muddied the lineage of Jesus. Her name here would only embarrass those who proclaimed Jesus as Israel's Messiah.

In fact, why mention women at all. This genealogy was a legal document, and women in the first century weren't legal heirs. They weren't even allowed to testify in a court of law. Other biblical genealogies list only fathers and sons and do not mention mothers at all.

But Matthew isn't through. Down in verse 5, we read that **Salmon was the father of Boaz** *by Rahab*. And who was Rahab? She wasn't someone who pretended to be a prostitute; she was, in fact, a career prostitute.

Rahab was rescued when her hometown of Jericho was destroyed by the Israelites. And she eventually married a prince from Israel. But even in Hebrews 11, her tagline reads "Rahab the harlot."

What's Matthew doing here? Why has he listed these women along with the various men in Jesus' genealogy?

First, not everyone will identify with the life of an Abraham, or even a Solomon or a David. Yes, they sinned too, sometimes grievously, but many people will more readily identify with a lowly sinner like Rahab.

Second, this is also a subtle reminder from Matthew that while it is easy to look at any sinner's past life, we should make sure we don't overlook the future life of the one who repents.

This leads us to one final observation from this genealogical list.

NO LOST SINNER IS UNREDEEMABLE

Rahab apparently was the only person in Jericho who was interested in the God of Israel. When the Israelite spies came to her, she acknowledged the Lord as "God in heaven above and on earth beneath" (Joshua 2:11), and she hid the spies on her rooftop.

Before the spies left her home and escaped from the city, they told her to hang a scarlet cord out her window. And when the Israelites came to that city, a city whose walls were about to come tumbling down, that scarlet cord would identify her and her family so that they would be spared.

The usual Hebrew word for a cord is bypassed in Joshua 2:18, which instead uses a word that can be translated "hope." Hope! Imagine this: Rahab had been hopeless, but now she staked everything on her hope in a forgiving, accepting God. So Rahab went from being a hopeless harlot to being a forgiven follower of God.

I recall preaching in the city of Medellin, Colombia. A government auditorium had been rented, and several thousand people were packed into it. In fact, many people were turned away an hour before the service began. I preached a simple gospel message on the incarnation and humility of Christ, and my translator invited people forward afterward, where counselors from neighboring churches were prepared to talk to them about the Lord. Several people believed the gospel and accepted Christ that evening.

An hour after the meeting when most of the people had finally left, one of the translators brought a woman up on stage. Evidently several people had invited her and had been praying that she would come that night.

She appeared to be in her late twenties or early thirties, and through a translator she began to talk to me. She told me she was a prostitute and a drug courier for one of the cartels in Colombia; but with tears in her eyes, she said she was leaving that life behind because she was now a follower of Jesus Christ.

I couldn't help but think of Rahab—what a past but, more so, what a future.

All of us who believe in Christ can testify that we were not too far away for the mercy and grace of God to reach us. Look at *your* past life . . . but don't stop there. Follow Him in your present life, and then try, just try, to imagine your future life with Him in heaven.

Chapter 3

The Song of Mary
Luke 1:26-56

Some of the most beautiful music ever composed centers on the incarnation of God the Son.

The prophet Isaiah penned the immortal words, "For a child will be born to us, a son will be given to us; and the government will rest on His shoulders" (Isaiah 9:6). You can almost hear the strains of Handel's *Messiah* in Isaiah's lyrics: "And His name will be called Wonderful Counselor, Mighty God, Eternal Father, Prince of Peace."

Not only did a prophet sing, but a priest sang as well. Once the tongue of Zacharias was loosened after the birth of his son John, he burst into a song he had been composing for nine months. He sang about the Sunrise from on high who would end the night of darkness and bring the dawn of everlasting peace (Luke 1:78-79).

Perhaps the youngest person to compose a hymn about the coming birth of Christ was a young woman named Mary, who was also visited by the angel Gabriel. Before we rush to the lyrics of Mary's hymn, however, let's look at the all-important events that gave rise to it.

MARY'S SETTING

Now in the sixth month the angel Gabriel was sent from God to a city in Galilee, called Nazareth. (Luke 1:26)

That's enough information to send shivers down the orthodox Jewish spine. Gabriel came with the most significant message ever delivered to the human race. He winged his way through the galaxies to Earth to deliver the news that Messiah was about to be born. And he came, not to Judea, where God had worked throughout the centuries, but instead came to Nazareth in Galilee.

Nazareth was polluted with Gentiles and Romans. It was unclean and of no real significance among the Jews. In fact, the rumor would eventually spread—and it's promoted by some to this day—that Mary had a dalliance with a Roman soldier and gave her baby the name Jesus.

When Nathanael was told about Christ and heard that Jesus was from Nazareth, he said, "Can any good thing come out of Nazareth?" (John 1:46). Nazareth was located on the other side of the tracks.

Furthermore, by going to Nazareth, Gabriel, as well as the God who sent him, was ignoring the holy city of Jerusalem and the most holy place in all of Israel, the temple.

Surely this news would be delivered in Israel's capital. Surely the mother of the Messiah would be one of the high priest's daughters or from one of the well-connected families of Jerusalem.

But Gabriel ignored the religious and the well bred. He flew on past the pious, the educated, and the homes thought most likely to raise the Messiah. Luke informs us that Gabriel instead went to Nazareth and **to a virgin engaged to a man whose name was Joseph, of the descendants of David; and the virgin's name was Mary** (Luke 1:27).

The greatest news ever announced on earth was delivered in the most unlikely city and to the most unlikely person. The recipient was a teenager who was as poverty stricken as those around her.

The one bright spot in Mary's life was that she was engaged to a man named Joseph. Neither was from a wealthy family. According to early church sources, Joseph made plows and yokes and other implements for the farmers living around him.

It is somewhat ironic to see that Joseph's (Matthew 1:1-17) and Mary's (Luke 3:23-38) family trees lead all the way back to David. This poverty-stricken couple were rightful heirs to the throne of their ancestor, King David himself. Joseph and Mary had royal blood flowing through their veins.

Still, as one author wrote:

> From all the indicators, [Mary's] life would not be extraordinary. She would marry humbly, give birth to numerous poor children . . . and one day die like thousands of others before her—a nobody in a nothing town in the middle of nowhere.[1]

To this day, the gospel seems to fly past the proud, the well connected, and the religious. But the gospel of the Messiah is still welcomed by people who know they are needy and unworthy.

In the same way, the Messiah was born to a young woman who never would have been considered worthy. She was just a poor girl who lived on the other side of the tracks. Life for Mary, however, was about to change forever.

MARY'S SURPRISE

And coming in, he said to her, "Greetings, favored one! The Lord is with you." But she was very perplexed at this statement, and kept pondering what kind of salutation this was. The angel said to her, "Do not be afraid, Mary; for you have found favor with God." (Luke 1:28-30)

The Latin Vulgate translated Gabriel's opening remarks in verse 28, "Hail Mary, full of grace." If the author Luke had wanted to communicate that Mary was full of grace, however, he would have used the same Greek expression he used in Acts 6:8, where he wrote that Stephen was full of God's grace.

Gabriel was simply telling Mary she had been chosen by God, that she had found favor with God, not because of what she had done for God, but because of what God was about to do for her!

The Vulgate's faulty translation implies that Mary was already filled with grace that she had merited on her own. This gave rise to the corruption within the Roman church during the Middle Ages, which claimed Mary had every gift, even above those given to angels. This view in turn gave rise to the idea that Mary could also be a dispenser of grace to humanity, which resulted in prayers being offered to her. These prayers often begin with the incorrect translation of the

Greek language into the Latin with the words, "Hail Mary, full of grace."

There are two extremes to which one can go in regard to Mary. One is to magnify her, and the other is to ignore her.

To magnify Mary above all other human beings is to effectively deify her. She would have to be divine in order to hear millions of prayers at the same time and then dispense grace as well as influence God.

Even further corrupt teaching began extolling Mary as someone who never sinned and thus was never in need of a Savior.

This was dogmatized on December 8, 1854, when Pope Pius IX declared the doctrine of the immaculate conception. The pope said, "From the first moment of her conception, the Blessed Virgin Mary was . . . kept free from stain of original sin."[2]

In other words, according to this teaching, Mary never sinned. In fact, she didn't have a sin nature; she was free from original sin.

The Bible never says anything like that. However, we do read that Jesus knew no sin (2 Cor. 5:21), committed no sin (1 Peter 2:22), and had no sin (1 John 3:5).

Gabriel did not come to explain to Mary how she had been able to live a perfect life, free from corruption; he came to explain how she would conceive by God's power and give flesh and blood to the Messiah.

While some magnify the servant rather than the Sovereign, others go to the opposite extreme of ignoring the servant. Their desire is to stay far away from the theological distortion that enlarges the role of Mary to co-redeemer and co-mediator. However, this can cause one to overlook an incredible young woman whose surrender to God is a model of submission and faith.

MARY'S SUBMISSION

> **"And behold, you will conceive in your womb and bear a son, and you shall name Him Jesus. He will be great and will be called the Son of the Most High; and the Lord God will give Him the throne of His father David; and He will reign over the house of Jacob forever, and His kingdom will have no end." Mary said to the angel, "How can this be, since I am a virgin?"** (Luke 1:31-34)

While our focus in this chapter is on Mary's response to God's message and her song of praise, it is important to grasp the enormity of what Gabriel promised her. He left no doubt that Mary was God's chosen vessel to bear Israel's long-awaited Messiah.

Gabriel just backed the prophetic truck up and unloaded. He made several prophetic statements here:

- Mary would conceive in her womb.

- She would bear a Son.

- She would name her Son Jesus.

- Jesus would be great.

- He would be the Son of God.

These five prophecies were fulfilled at Christ's first coming.

The next three prophecies in Gabriel's truckload will come to pass at Christ's second coming.

- God the Father will give to God the Son the throne of His earthly forefather David.

- Jesus will reign over Israel forever.

- His kingdom will never end.

Here are eight rapid-fire, centuries-sweeping prophecies that begin with Mary's pregnancy and end with the eternal state of heaven.

Gabriel's words must have seemed overwhelming to Mary. As she tried to process what they meant, she seemed to focus on the first prediction: **"You will conceive in your womb."**

Her first response was, **"How can this be, since I am a virgin?"** This appears to be amazingly similar to the reaction of Zacharias back in verse 18, when Gabriel appeared to him and told him his wife, Elizabeth, would bear a son in her old age. Zacharias said to the angel, "How will I know this for certain? For I am an old man and my wife is advanced in years." There was an important difference between their questions, however.

Zacharias responded with doubt and demanded proof. He essentially said, "I need a sign in order to believe." As a result, he was disciplined for his unbelief.

Mary, however, was not rebuked for her question simply because she wasn't doubting the angelic promise; she just didn't understand the physical process!

Gabriel answered Mary's question in verse 35.

The angel answered and said to her, "The Holy Spirit will come upon you, and the power of the Most High will overshadow you; and for that reason the holy Child shall be called the Son of God."

That word translated **overshadow** is the same word used in the Greek Old Testament to refer to the presence of God in the Holy of Holies in the Jewish tabernacle and later the temple. "Mary's womb became a holy of holies for the Son of God."[3]

After Gabriel encouraged Mary with the news that her elderly relative Elizabeth was in her sixth month of pregnancy, Mary responded to the angel in verse 38.

And Mary said, "Behold, the bondslave of the Lord; may it be done to me according to your word." And the angel departed from her.

Did Mary's submission eventually lead her to inform Joseph? It's quite possible she did tell him and tried to explain that she was not pregnant by another man but that an angel had visited her and told her she would conceive supernaturally. If so, Joseph didn't believe her.

It is difficult for us to imagine the grief in both their hearts. To Joseph, the woman he had planned to marry had been unfaithful. To Mary, the man she had planned to marry no longer trusted her.

But Joseph still loved Mary. Matthew tells us he didn't want to disgrace her publicly, so he planned to put her away privately.

However, Joseph was visited by an angel during a dream. The angel confirmed that Mary had conceived miraculously through the work of the Holy Spirit. Joseph was also informed that he was to marry her and give the newborn baby the name Jesus (*Savior*), because He would save His people from their sins.

Would anyone else possibly believe this strange story besides Joseph and Mary? Their families wouldn't. Their neighbors wouldn't. The nation of Israel wouldn't.

The Talmud (a collection of Jewish law and commentary) would later suggest that Mary was the mistress of Panthera, a Roman soldier, and thus Jesus would be considered illegitimate. In fact, even when Christ began His ministry, the Pharisees said to Him in John 8:41, "We were not born of fornication." Their implication was that He was born out of wedlock.

Gabriel's revelation to Mary pointed her to some who would believe her story: an old couple named Elizabeth and Zacharias. Mary hurried to their home, probably a good three days' journey away. As soon as Mary arrived, Elizabeth's unborn son leaped in her womb in recognition of the One Mary carried in her womb. Mary and Elizabeth enjoyed fellowship that only such mothers could enjoy—one, the mother of John the Baptist, the forerunner to the Messiah, the other, the mother of Jesus, the Messiah.

MARY'S SONG

Mary began to sing the song she must have been composing over her three-day journey. Look at what she praised God for in her song.

She Praised God for Her Salvation

"My soul exalts the Lord, and my spirit has rejoiced in God my Savior." (Luke 1:46-47)

Don't ever forget, *Mary* needed a Savior too. Like all of humanity, Mary needed to be redeemed.

This thought is presented in the words of another, more recent song that declares that the One Mary delivered would soon deliver *her*![4]

She Praised God for Her Testimony

"For He has had regard for the humble state of His bondslave; for behold, from this time on all generations will count me blessed." (Luke 1:48)

Mary was in effect saying, "Imagine that God would choose someone like me to do something like this!"

She Praised God for His Power

"For the Mighty One has done great things for me; and holy is His name." (Luke 1:49)

She Praised God for His Mercy

"AND HIS MERCY IS UPON GENERATION AFTER GEN-
ERATION TOWARD THOSE WHO FEAR HIM." (Luke
1:50)

She Praised God for His Sovereignty

Mary gave praise to God for displaying His sovereignty
in at least three different ways.

By Exalting the Humble

"He has done mighty deeds with His arm;
He has scattered those who were proud in the
thoughts of their heart. He has brought down
rulers from their thrones, and has exalted
those who were humble." (Luke 1:51-52)

By Enriching the Hungry

"HE HAS FILLED THE HUNGRY WITH GOOD THINGS;
and sent away the rich empty-handed." (Luke
1:53)

By Establishing the Helpless

"He has given help to Israel His servant, in re-
membrance of His mercy, as He spoke to our
fathers, to Abraham and his descendants forever." (Luke 1:54-55)

As you study this hymn, you may notice that almost every
phrase is a quotation from or allusion to the Old Testament
Scriptures. Mary apparently had faithfully memorized many

of the passages of the Old Testament she had been taught as a child.

Mary's thoughts of God were high and wonderful. The God she worshipped is able to save. He is merciful, holy, and powerful. He is also sovereign in His management of the world, exalting the humble, enriching the hungry, and establishing the helpless.

CONCLUSION

In verse 56, we read:

**And Mary stayed with her about three months,
and then returned to her home.**

I've heard it suggested that when Mary returned to Nazareth she essentially sailed into a storm that would last the rest of her life. The truth is, that storm has continued to this day, two thousand years later.

The most difficult times to sing are the difficult times. Mary sang in a difficult time, but her song says nothing of life back in Nazareth. It offers no answer to Mary's pain or coming sorrow. Rather, her lyrics focus on God her Savior, who is sovereign and merciful.

The true Christmas Carol is sung by all those who, like Mary, place their faith in the sovereign Son of God.

Chapter 4

The Surrender of Bliss
Matthew 1:18-25

Wilmer McLean was a retired grocer who had bought a beautiful estate near Manassas Junction in Virginia and settled into plantation life. McLean refused to participate in the Civil War.

Unfortunately for him, the first major battle in the Civil War occurred at Manassas Junction on July 21, 1861. The First Battle of Manassas, also known as the Battle of Bull Run, saw some 50,000 soldiers engaged in a fight that lasted all day. This was the famous battle where General Thomas Jackson earned his nickname "Stonewall" for his unwillingness to back down.

And where did Stonewall Jackson do some of his fighting? On Wilmer McLean's plantation.

When the battle was over, McLean's buildings had been destroyed. A cannonball actually went down the chimney of his home. Even his beautiful stone barn was demolished.

McLean wanted nothing to do with this war, yet the war had found him, and it cost him nearly everything. Wilmer McLean decided to move 120 miles south, where he bought a house in an out-of-the-way place called Appomattox Court House, Virginia.

Poor guy. That's exactly where one of the last battles of the war was fought four years later. In fact, it was the place where General Robert E. Lee and General Ulysses S. Grant signed the terms of surrender. They needed a place to meet and agree to the terms. They chose to meet in the parlor of the home of Wilmer McLean.

And so, on April 9, 1865, the meeting took place in McLean's parlor. It lasted two and a half hours, and when it was over and the generals had departed, Union soldiers, wanting mementos of this once-in-a-lifetime event, took pictures from his walls, silverware and settings, furniture, and even the drapes. When it was over and the people were gone, nearly everything from Wilmer McLean's home was gone.

Wilmer McLean just wanted to steer clear of the Civil War, but it seemed to hunt him down. It started in his backyard and ended in his parlor. And it cost him nearly everything.

Poor Wilmer McLean. He longed to stay uninvolved and out of sight, but the war boxed him in, and there was no place to run.

Ask the average Christian what his or her perspective is of the Christmas narrative and Joseph's involvement, and more than likely the mere mention of his name will evoke pity. Poor Joseph. He just couldn't stay out of harm's way. He got engaged to a girl and planned to get married, have children, and expand his carpentry business, and wham! Suddenly, he was right in the middle of something that would turn his world upside down.

The average person thinks of Joseph as an unwilling or barely willing participant who is somewhat out of the picture.

He is like a schoolchild in the Christmas play who's dazzled into mute silence by the spotlight and the sight of the crowd. Joseph seemed to be thrust into the spotlight of human history for a brief moment, and then he was gone.

Have you ever noticed the Christmas plays? Joseph's the guy who leads the donkey around and then knocks on the innkeeper's door and asks, "Is there any room?" He might have a couple more lines in the stable scene, and that's about it.

The truth is, Joseph did much more than lead the donkey around and fluff up the hay in the manger.

As much as anyone in the original Christmas carol, Joseph modeled self-sacrifice. He demonstrated what it means when we dare say to God, "I surrender all." Joseph was essentially willing to say farewell to the bliss of a simple, peaceful life. And in his surrender, Joseph provides us with a model worthy of imitation.

A MODEL OF SURRENDER

Surrender of Personal Pride

Now the birth of Jesus Christ was as follows: when His mother Mary had been betrothed to Joseph, before they came together she was found to be with child by the Holy Spirit. And Joseph her husband, being a righteous man and not wanting to disgrace her, planned to send her away secretly. (Matthew 1:18-19)

51

In order to understand the devastating blow Mary's pregnancy was to Joseph, we need to understand something about the Jewish wedding customs of that day.

There were three stages to a Jewish wedding. The first stage was called the *engagement*. This was an agreement the parents made while the children were younger. Parents normally picked out the spouses for their children. Sometimes, the couple never met until the second stage.

The second stage was called the betrothal period, or the *kiddushin*. This involved a formal pledge of marriage that was legally binding. During a brief ceremony, the bridegroom would pay the dowry, or the *mohar*. This was the bride price. It was often paid in cattle or clothing or money or all three, depending on the wealth of the bridegroom. It was given to the bride's father to compensate him for wedding expenses.[1]

The *kiddushin* lasted a year. During this period, the couple didn't live together or consummate their marriage. The bridegroom would spend this year preparing a home for his bride.

The analogy to our Lord Jesus Christ, our Bridegroom, is both illuminating and thrilling. Our Bridegroom paid the price for us, His bride, with His own blood, and now we await the time when He'll return for us and take us to the home He's prepared for us (John 14:2). We're already His beloved, and His Spirit is our seal/engagement ring (2 Corinthians 1:21-22; Ephesians 1:13); our wedding feast, the "marriage supper of the Lamb" (Revelation 19:9), is just ahead, occurring in heaven in the near future.

In Joseph and Mary's day, the *kiddushin* was binding. They were actually considered husband and wife, legally married, even though they had not yet reached the third stage of ceremony and consummation.

The only way out of a betrothal was death or divorce. In fact, had Joseph died during the betrothal period, Mary would have been considered a *widow*.

The betrothal period was a time when both man and woman prepared themselves for their life together. The man would be busily preparing a dwelling place, and the woman would be collecting all the things necessary to be a wife, a homemaker, and a helper for her husband.[2]

The third and final stage was called the *huppah*. This was the actual wedding ceremony. It involved several days of feasting and celebrating the goodness of God in establishing another household of faith.

Now, with this background, consider the devastation to Joseph:

> **When . . . Mary had been betrothed to Joseph, before they came together she was found to be with child.**

How could this be? In Luke's Gospel we're told that an angel visited Mary and explained what was going to happen. Joseph didn't have that benefit.

Matthew 1:19 describes Joseph as Mary's **husband**, reminding us of the legally binding relationship he had with Mary. What could he possibly do?

Joseph could bring her before the elders and accuse her of sexual sin with another man. This would keep him from the obvious accusation that he was the culprit, that he couldn't wait until the *kiddushin* was past, that he was the child's father.

Joseph had a godly reputation that was now on the verge of being destroyed. He could clear his name by bringing a public charge against Mary. Mary would pay the consequences for her sin, and he could try to get on with his life. It would have been perfectly understandable—and acceptable—for Joseph to take such action.

The text tells us that Joseph was **a righteous man**. The Greek word for righteous refers to the heart as well as the conduct.[3] Joseph desired to do the right thing, but he also loved Mary, and so, **not wanting to disgrace her, he planned to send her away secretly**.

The rabbinical writings allowed a man in Joseph's position to either accuse the woman publicly or divorce her as quietly as possible. Joseph had decided upon the latter. All he needed were two witnesses, and the *kiddushin* was over.

Joseph at this moment chose compassion over emotion, discretion over revenge. Discretion is knowing when to keep silent in spite of emotion.

It's one thing to remain quiet when *you* are wrong; it's difficult to remain quiet when you've been wronged. And it's especially hard to remain quiet when you're right!

Perhaps our greatest test of character is knowing when to remain silent rather than proving we are right.

Joseph intended to quietly break off the betrothal without any public humiliation for Mary, even though doing the latter would have vindicated his own reputation.

Don't miss the fact that the will of God for Joseph involved breaking his heart.

Surrender of Personal Privacy

But when he had considered this, behold, an angel of the Lord appeared to him in a dream, saying, "Joseph, son of David, do not be afraid to take Mary as your wife; for the Child who has been conceived in her is of the Holy Spirit." (Matthew 1:20)

God was asking Joseph not only to surrender his pride but also to surrender his privacy.

The Lord's message to Joseph included an implicit warning that his life would never be the same; his obedience to God would launch him into the public spotlight for the rest of his life.

He was about to become the Messiah's stepfather; responsible to raise this miraculously conceived, virgin-born Savior.

Shortly after the birth of Christ, Joseph got a taste of how much his life would change. Shepherds showed up unannounced to worship Jesus, delivering to the couple the news that a host of angels had appeared in the sky chanting the news of the Savior's birth.

Two years later, Joseph's home would be visited by dignitaries from the land of Persia, magi who came bringing costly gifts and honoring the King of the Jews. Imagine the commotion in Bethlehem.

We know from Scripture that Joseph was given revelation through dreams at least four times. Three times, perhaps within three years, he relocated his family, reestablished his carpentry business, and set up their home. We also know that in the early years of parenting Jesus, they were virtually running for their lives.

What a whirlwind!

Joseph no doubt longed for that quiet village life he once knew. While he may have wanted life to go back to the way it had been in Nazareth, he knew that would never happen.

The will of God would be inconvenient, uncomfortable, surprising, dangerous, tiring, confusing, and demanding. Farewell, Joseph, to the bliss of a quiet life.

What has God asked you to surrender for His Son? Joseph responded with affirmation when God asked him to sacrifice his pride and his privacy.

Surrender of Personal Priorities

"She will bear a Son; and you shall call His name Jesus, for He will save His people from their sins." Now all this took place to fulfill what was spoken by the Lord through the prophet: "BEHOLD, THE VIRGIN SHALL BE WITH CHILD AND SHALL BEAR A SON, AND THEY SHALL CALL HIS NAME IMMANUEL," which translated means, "GOD WITH US." (Matthew 1:21-23)

The angel was emphasizing again that the Son born to Mary would be the Messiah, the Savior of the world. The words regarding the fulfillment of the prophecy in Isaiah 7:14 are probably Matthew's explanation rather than the words of the angel to Joseph, but they stress that all Joseph and Mary were experiencing was part of God's grand plan. Joseph would be responsible to care for and train the Savior.

No doubt Joseph would struggle with a great sense of inadequacy. Where's the parenting manual for raising the Messiah?

Here was a man who had little if any formal education, yet he would be responsible to educate the greatest educator of all time.

The Jewish customs regarding the education of children were fairly clear. We know that from the time a boy turned three till he reached the age of twelve, the father was responsible to pass down to him the traditions, customs, ordinances, and laws of God. What an intimidating assignment this was for Joseph.

We must understand that Jesus' mind wasn't already downloaded with biblical software. Luke tells us that he grew in wisdom (Luke 2:40, 52).

I can imagine Joseph saying, "Me? God, You want me to teach the prophecies of Scripture to the One who is the fulfillment of prophecy? You want me to teach the law to the One who will fulfill the law? You want me to teach the system of worship and sacrifices to the One who is the final sacrifice? Why not Joseph of Arimathea? Why me, Joseph of Nazareth?"

We know from history that both Josephs lived at the same time in Israel. Joseph of Arimathea was a wealthy man, able to afford tutors for his children. He was a member of the Sanhedrin, the Jewish supreme court; he knew the law like the back of his hand. The Bible tells us that he was also a righteous man, looking for the kingdom of God (Luke 23:50-51; Mark 15:43). He would have made a great father for the Messiah.

Did the names somehow get switched? No. Just as God chose who *your* parents would be and who *your* children would be, God chose Joseph of Nazareth and a teenage girl named Mary to raise Jesus, the Messiah.

THE NATURE OF SURRENDER

In studying this scene, especially in relation to the life of Joseph, two principles emerge regarding the nature of godly surrender.

Surrender Means Sacrifice

"Here, Lord, use my house. Move into my parlor! You can have my drapes, my silverware, my property. You can put my education to use for Your glory. You can have my children and my car keys. You can have access to my calendar, my schedule, my wallet, and my career. You can take control of my *life*."

I wonder how many Christians shuttle between northern Virginia and southern Virginia in an attempt to avoid the battle—anything but engage in the cause of Christ to advance His name.

A few years ago, a full-page ad ran in the North Carolina State University school newspaper.

The headline read, "This Christmas Card was written 500 years before Christmas." It then went on to explain:

About 500 years before Jesus' birth, the prophet Micah wrote that the Messiah would be born in Bethlehem, right where Jesus was born.[4] And do you know who knew of Micah's prophecy? All the religious leaders who advised King Herod. We're told that when Jesus was born, some wise men from the East went to King Herod in Jerusalem. They asked Herod where the Messiah was born, "For we have seen his star in the east, and have come to worship him." Herod didn't know. So he gathered all the chief priests and scribes and asked them where the Christ was to be born. They told him, "In Bethlehem of Judea; for so it is written by the prophet . . ." There are over a hundred such prophecies that describe who this Messiah would be and what he would do—like a prophetic Global Positioning Satellite pointing out the Messiah, the Christ. The amazing thing is that Jesus fulfilled every one of them. Before the end of the first century countless Jews and Gentiles in the Middle East put their faith in Him. This Christmas is a good time for you to look at the life and teaching of Jesus and decide for yourself. A good place to start is by asking God to reveal the truth to you—He will. Open to the section of the Bible called "John" and begin reading.

The rest of the page was filled with names. I counted about 120 professors and staff listed in this ad. And so readers could find them, the department where each one served was listed next to each name.

If this weren't enough, just above the names in a larger font was a paragraph that read:

> This ad is sponsored by the following NC State Faculty and Staff who are followers of Jesus Christ. If you have any questions about what it would be like to have a personal relationship with Him, feel free to drop by our offices and talk.

Isn't that great? But such a public statement involves sacrifice. In this case, it may have meant the sacrifice of a promotion or professional credibility. Why risk the inconvenience? Why threaten your career path? Why ask for misunderstanding and even ridicule?

As it was for Joseph, surrendering to the will of God is about sacrifice, not convenience.

Surrender Means Obedience

How many giants did King David kill before he stood in front of Goliath? None.

How many Messiahs did Joseph raise before kneeling over a manger in Bethlehem? None.

God isn't looking for experience but readiness, willingness, and obedience.

Perhaps the most significant words in Matthew 1—at least in regard to this man Joseph—are these:

And Joseph awoke from his sleep and did as the angel of the Lord commanded him, and took Mary as his wife, but kept her a virgin

until she gave birth to a Son; and he called His name Jesus. (Matthew 1:24-25)

It was as simple as that: Joseph obeyed the word of God.

But make no mistake, that decision would cost him *everything*.

When Joseph folded his blanket and put on his tunic that morning, he said farewell to the bliss of a predictable life. He handed God his pride, his plans, his priorities, his dreams, his options, and his calendar, and he said the same thing his adopted Son would one day say, "Not my will, but Yours be done."

Chapter 5

From Riches to Rags

Luke 2:1-7

If you had been alive in 1809, you would have considered Napoleon's battles in Austria the most significant thing happening in the civilized world. The last place you would have thought to be significant or important was the backwoods of Kentucky, where in 1809, a poor, illiterate wandering laborer's wife delivered a newborn baby named Abraham Lincoln. Certainly, the birth of a boy in Hardin County, Kentucky, seemed insignificant to the world, whose destiny was in the hands of a French dictator and emerging world ruler named Napoleon . . . or was it?

If you had been alive two thousand years ago, the eyes of the world would have been focused on the empire of Rome and its emerging leader. After defeating Antony and Cleopatra's bid for the throne of Rome, he had solidified the Roman Empire and become its first true emperor.

His given name was Gaius Octavian. But after assuming the throne of his deceased great uncle, Julius Caesar, he also assumed the title of Caesar. Caesar was simply a generic title given to the emperor.

The Roman senate, however, also voted to give Caesar Octavian the title Augustus. Augustus meant "revered" or "holy," and up to this time had been used exclusively of the gods. Thus, two thousand years ago, the belief was established that the Roman Caesar was the son of the gods.

Historians have said that Caesar Augustus was probably Rome's greatest leader. Legend has it that with his last words he boasted, "I found Rome a city of bricks and left it a city of marble." An inscription discovered in the ancient city of Halicarnassus refers to him as "savior of the whole world."[1]

Two thousand years ago, the spotlight never would have shifted to the village of Nazareth. Nobody would have ever thought to look at a baby born to peasant parents in Bethlehem as having any significance or influence over the future of the world.

That birth would be ignored entirely by Rome. And why not?

How could another peasant boy born in Palestine compare with Caesar Augustus of Rome, the powerful emperor who was declared the son of the gods and the savior of the world?

The prophet Isaiah said of Christ, "He has no stately form or majesty that we should look upon Him . . . He was despised . . . and we did not esteem Him" (Isaiah 53:2-3). That's another way of saying, "We looked at Him and never would have guessed in a million years that He was anyone important."

Caesar Augustus looked like a son of the gods ought to look. Behind him stood all the splendor and wealth of Rome! Behind Jesus Christ stood only poverty and lowliness of the lowest class. To the world, Jesus doesn't look anything like a Son of God!

Why did Jesus Christ come to earth the way He did? Why was He surrounded by poverty? Paul answered that question when he wrote these words about Christ to the Corinthian believers: "Though He was rich, yet for your sake He became poor, so that you through His poverty might become rich" (2 Corinthians 8:9).

There were two predominant words translated "poor" in the Greek world. One word referred to someone who had just enough money to pay off his bills and buy his food. After he paid his debts and bought enough food to survive, he was out of money. He was poor until his next paycheck.

But there was another word translated "poor," the word *ptōchos.* It referred to someone who never had money to begin with. This was the person who couldn't pay his bills and didn't have any money for food; he was living in abject poverty, totally impoverished. He never ran out of money because he didn't have any to run out of—he had none to spend or save or even lose.

Paul used the verb form of the word *ptōchos* in 2 Corinthians 8:9. This was the kind of poor person Jesus Christ became. In this verse Paul was thinking of the entirety of the incarnation. He was saying, "For your sakes, the totality of the event of Christ becoming man was impoverishment. It was choosing abject poverty so that believers could one day inherit eternal glory."

Jesus went from riches to rags so that we could go from rags to riches. He came from heaven to earth so that we could go from earth to heaven.

Let's travel back now to the time when the Son of God was born on Earth, when Immanuel, "God with us," would begin playing the first strains of the original Christmas carol.

THE MIGHTY HAND OF GOD

Now in those days a decree went out from Caesar Augustus, that a census be taken of all the inhabited earth. This was the first census taken while Quirinius was governor of Syria. (Luke 2:1-2)

Caesar ordered a census of his entire empire. The purpose was to register people for the collection of taxes. Whether Jew or Gentile, they were to go to the town of their lineage and register there. This would have included giving their name, occupation, children's names, and so on.

In times like these, it must have seemed like Caesar Augustus was in control of the events of the world. But nothing could be further from the truth.

In reality Augustus was God's errand boy, delivering a decree at precisely the right moment. Had he issued his decree three months earlier or three months later, Mary's Child would have been born in Nazareth. But this could not be, for Scripture had prophesied His birth in Bethlehem, and God worked through the pagan emperor to ensure that prophecy was fulfilled.

God was orchestrating everything to fulfill His sovereign will and His eternal word. The Word of God had prophesied that:

- The Redeemer would be a human being (Genesis 3:15)

- The Savior would be a Jew, not a Gentile (Genesis 12:1-3)

- The Savior would come from the tribe of Judah (Genesis 49:10)

- The Messiah would be a descendant of David (2 Samuel 7:1-17)

- The Messiah would be born of a virgin (Isaiah 7:14)

- Jesus would be born in Bethlehem (Micah 5:2)

All those prophecies were fulfilled when Jesus was born of the Virgin Mary in the very village also prophesied to be His birthplace.

THE HUMBLE CITY OF DAVID

Hundreds of years before the birth of Christ, the prophet Micah provided the original address of the Messiah:

> But as for you, Bethlehem Ephrathah, too little to be among the clans of Judah, from you One will go forth for Me to be ruler in Israel. His goings forth are from long ago, from the days of eternity. (Micah 5:2)

It might have looked like Caesar was calling the shots. It might have looked like Mary and Joseph were helpless pawns caught up in the politics of taxes and world rulers, but in reality every move was perfectly timed and directed by the hand of God.

Luke continues the narrative in verses 3-5:

And everyone was on his way to register for the census, each to his own city. Joseph also went up from Galilee, from the city of Nazareth, to Judea, to the city of David which is called Bethlehem, because he was of the house and family of David, in order to register along with Mary, who was engaged to him, and was with child.

In accordance with the decree of Caesar Augustus, Joseph left Nazareth in Galilee and traveled to his ancestral home of Bethlehem in Judea. Mary, nearing the end of her pregnancy, wasn't about to stay behind, and no doubt Joseph wasn't about to leave her behind.

Interestingly, while Mary accompanied Joseph to Bethlehem, she is said here to have been **engaged** to Joseph. Matthew 1:24, however, says that Joseph "took Mary as his wife," apparently well before the events of Luke 2. Luke's expression probably is emphasizing the fact that while they lived together as husband and wife, the marriage had not yet been consummated as Matthew 1:25 explains.

Bethlehem literally means "house of bread." In John 6:35, Jesus calls Himself "the bread of life." There was no better place for the Bread of Life to be born than in the "house of bread."

Bethlehem was where the patriarch Jacob buried his wife Rachel after she died in childbirth. And those fields that Mary and Joseph passed by were the same fields where Ruth once had gathered wheat and was noticed by Boaz. This is the same little village where David tended the family sheep before he was chosen to be the next king of Israel.

These were the relatives of Joseph and Mary. Had there been a legitimate Jewish king on the throne in Jerusalem in their day, he would have been related to Joseph and Mary. Both were the descendants of David—Joseph through David's son Solomon and Mary through David's son Nathan. This means that their Son could be the rightful prince of David, the King of Israel.

But the world didn't even notice. It was impressed with mighty Rome, not little Bethlehem. Despite its rich history, Bethlehem was not considered of great importance, even in Joseph and Mary's day. The prophet Micah spoke of the town as "too little to be among the clans of Judah," as if to say it was not even worthy to be put on a map.

THE LOWLY BIRTH OF THE SON

While they were there, the days were completed for her to give birth. And she gave birth to her firstborn son; and she wrapped Him in cloths, and laid Him in a manger, because there was no room for them in the inn. (Luke 2:6-7)

Some things haven't changed. The inn was overcrowded then, and the hearts of people are overcrowded today. There is still no room for Jesus today.

Did Joseph argue with the innkeeper? We have no indication that he did. We're simply told that the inn was full, and it's not God's way to pull strings and drop names. Indeed,

God had a very different plan anyway, and His plan involved a stable.

Justin Martyr, the second-century church leader, stated that the specific birthplace of Jesus was in a shallow cave used as a shelter for animals, which was common practice in those days. It's interesting that in the middle of the fourth century, the Emperor Constantine ordered that a church be built over the supposed birthplace of Christ, and it was built over and against a Bethlehem cave.

Whether it was a wooden stable or a cave in a Bethlehem hillside, we need to erase from our minds the Christmas card picture of fresh hay and clean animals and a warm fire. In fact, the last thing you'd ever want to do is build a fire in a stable around horses and donkeys.

That place may well have been dark and cold. We can imagine the night air being punctuated by Mary's cries of pain. Surrounded by manure and the stench of animals, the ground would have been packed hard or, worse yet, muddied by some recent rain.

I'm sure Joseph made Mary a soft place to lie down, perhaps with his own cloak. Her labor might have lasted well into the night. Perhaps Joseph held her hand, tried to encourage her, and shooed away the animals, wondering why it was happening like this and not knowing exactly what to do.

If you've had children, you might remember the uncertainty and fear that surrounded the birth of that first child. It was a new experience. Only here there were no nurses, doctors, midwives, or mothers or sisters to help—not a friend in sight. Luke simply records in verse 7, **And she gave birth to her firstborn son.**

Jesus was not her *only* son. In Matthew 13:55-56 Mary and Joseph's other sons, four in all, are introduced to us by name, along with unnamed daughters.

But Jesus was the **firstborn**, which meant he had the legal rights of inheritance. His mother and adoptive father were both descendants of King David. Jesus thus inherited the right to claim the throne of David and could be crowned the rightful King.

But for now, in that cave that reeked of livestock and dirty hay, this Baby seemed like anything but a king.

One author wrote,

> His face is prunish and red. His cry, though strong and healthy, is still the helpless and piercing cry of a baby. . . . Majesty in the midst of the mundane. Holiness in the filth of sheep manure and sweat. Divinity entering the world on the floor of a stable, through the womb of a teenager and in the presence of a carpenter.[2]

There was no halo circling the head of Jesus, and the animals didn't kneel and worship him. He looked, sounded, and felt like an ordinary baby. And after Mary **wrapped him** with strips of cloth, she laid her newborn baby in a **manger**. The Greek word for **manger** is *phatne*, which can literally be translated "feed trough." More than likely, as was the custom, it was a place cut into the stone along the side of the cave and then hollowed out to form a trough. Joseph evidently cleaned out a section of the trough and put a blanket or hay in it to cushion the Baby, and then he laid in that feed trough the Son of God.

A more wretched place to be born than this could not have been chosen. One could not have scripted a more humble, poverty-stricken beginning than this.

What a picture of God's condescension this is. He left behind the wealth of heaven and chose the rags of humanity. He entered the world of sin—that stable perhaps serving as a poignant metaphor for the filth of sinful humanity, which now surrounded Him.

Author Philip Yancey contrasted the humility that characterized Jesus' coming to earth with the typical visit by the British royal family to another country.

> Queen Elizabeth II had recently visited the United States, and reporters delighted in spelling out the logistics involved: her four thousand pounds of luggage included two outfits for every occasion, a mourning outfit in case someone died, forty pints of plasma, and white kid leather toilet seat covers. She brought along her own hairdresser, two valets, and a host of other attendants. A brief visit of royalty to a foreign country can easily cost twenty million dollars.
>
> In meek contrast, God's visit to earth took place in an animal shelter with no attendants present and nowhere to lay the newborn king but a feed trough.[3]

Why did the Lord give up His royal privileges? Why did He give all personal rights away? He did it so that He could give us the opportunity to claim the greatest right of all: "But as many as received Him, to them He gave *the right* to become children of God" (John 1:12).

Jesus couldn't have stooped any lower. Immanuel, God with us, had come from riches to rags. He became totally impoverished, so that through His poverty, we might become eternally enriched.

No wonder we love singing Christmas carols so much.

Chapter 6

The Announcement

Luke 2:8-20

In the early 1830s, two different groups of men, one in America and one in England, were independently racing to build an electric telegraph system.

Ultimately, the American group won the day with its unique use of magnetic pulses and a special code invented by the group's leader, Samuel Morse. By occupation, Morse was a skilled painter who specialized in portraits, but his invention took the world by storm, and by the late 1800s, electric telegraph companies were in operation.

Imagine, little more than 150 years ago, the fastest way for someone on the East Coast to get a message to someone living on the West Coast was the Pony Express. Mounted riders could relay the mail to its destination on the other coast in ten days. With the invention of the telegraph and the creation of the Morse code, that distance could be spanned at nearly the speed of light.

The first official telegram was dated May 24, 1844. On that historic day, Samuel Morse made the first public demonstration of his telegraph by sending a message from the Supreme Court chamber in the U. S. Capitol to a station in Baltimore. His famous message was only four words: "What hath God wrought." With those words, Samuel Morris gave his Creator

God the credit. In other words, he was saying, "Look at what God has done!"

Nearly two thousand years ago, God delivered a special message to Earth. His message did not come by way of a telegram or a letter, however. He delivered it by means of angels. I guess we could call it an "angelgram." What better way than angels for God to deliver the announcement of Jesus' birth in Bethlehem?

Back in their hometown of Nazareth, if everything had gone according to plan—which it obviously hadn't —the birth of a son would have been cause for celebration. Joseph and Mary would call all their friends and relatives together to celebrate the birth of their baby boy. In fact, the custom was for the father to hire musicians to come to the home and play music.

Instead, they were in a cave in Bethlehem, and they couldn't have felt more alone. They swaddled their Baby with strips of cloth, and their cradle was Joseph's cloak or perhaps some fresh straw arranged in the corner of a feeding trough.

There were no friends to celebrate with them and congratulate them. And there certainly were no musicians in sight.

But then again, God the Father had arranged for some musicians after all—not to mention a host of new friends.

UNLIKELY RECIPIENTS

In the same region there were some shepherds staying out in the fields and keeping watch over their flock by night. (Luke 2:8)

76

The announcement that the Son of God had been born—which is recorded in the verses that follow—was first made to shepherds. It is absolutely astounding that they were the first to find out.

Why is this so astonishing? First, consider whom God *disregarded*.

If you were assigned the public relations challenge of announcing the birth of God the Son, you would begin by making a list of everyone who ought to know. Then you would make sure everyone on the list somehow found out.

But God disregarded everyone and anyone that ought to have been on the list! He bypassed the educated, the religious, the elite, the politically connected, the wealthy, and the powerful. He didn't announce it to the Jewish supreme court, the Sanhedrin; He didn't announce it to the high priest at the temple in Jerusalem; He didn't have somebody send a memo to Caesar Augustus and the Roman senate.

Second, consider whom **God** *dignified*. Shepherds were the most unlikely people to be given the news of Christ's birth.

In Jesus' day, the only people considered socially more distasteful than shepherds were lepers. Shepherds weren't able to keep all the regulations of the scribes and Pharisees, such as washing their hands at certain times and avoiding dead animals.

According to the Mishnah, the Jewish writings that codified scribal law, shepherds were under an ongoing ban. They were considered perpetually unclean and therefore couldn't worship or enter the temple precinct.

In addition, shepherds worked on the Sabbath. The sheep didn't take Saturday off, so neither could the shepherds.

Shepherds were, by occupation, religious outcasts. Yet they were the *first* to hear the news of Jesus' nearby birth.

Clearly, the Bible has a much higher view of shepherds than did the Jewish leaders of Jesus' time. In fact, Jesus willingly referred to Himself as "the good shepherd" (John 10:11). Likewise, the apostle Peter called Jesus "the Chief Shepherd" (1 Peter 5:4), and Hebrews 13:20 calls Jesus "the great Shepherd of the sheep."

In the Bible, the title "shepherd" is given to elders who serve, lead, and feed Christ's church. In Ephesians 4:11, the word translated "pastors" is the word for shepherds, or literally, *feeders* who pasture the flock.

It must have seemed ironic in the first century for men who led the church in worship to be given the title of those who were never allowed to worship in the temple.

Another evidence of the low regard in which shepherds were held is that they were not allowed to be witnesses in any Jewish court of law. They were considered unreliable because they were not men of the temple. They were unclean and thus considered unworthy of bearing testimony before men.

God chose shepherds to be the first to testify to His Son's birth. We cannot miss the grace of God here, even at the very outset of His Son's life.

Look at those He disregarded! Look at those He dignified!

Luke further informs us that these shepherds were in the vicinity of Bethlehem, **keeping watch over their flock**

by night. Bethlehem was only six miles south of Jerusalem, essentially on the rural outskirts of the Holy City.

During Passover, Jerusalem grew to two to three million people as Jews came from all over with their lambs to sacrifice in celebration of their former deliverance from Egypt.

Exodus 12 tells us of the judgment the Lord brought upon Egypt, through the killing of the firstborn of every family, including Pharaoh's family. The only way the Israelites could escape this judgment was to put a lamb's blood on the door frames of their homes, which they did that night. Those who had the blood of the lamb smeared on their door frames were passed over by the plague of death. Passover was the annual celebration of that historic event.

The first-century Jewish historian Josephus records that during the lifetime of Jesus, around 250,000 lambs were killed and eaten at Jerusalem's annual Passover Feast.

Where did all those sheep come from? Many people raised their own, of course, but the temple authorities also raised sheep and other animals, which they sold to worshippers who came to the temple without an animal to sacrifice.

More than likely, these shepherds near Bethlehem were on the temple payroll watching flocks of sheep kept for Jewish sacrifices. In fact, the Mishnah declared that any animal found between Jerusalem and Bethlehem was destined for sacrifice in the temple of Jerusalem.

These shepherds, then, were quite likely keeping watch over sheep that would be sacrificed on the temple altar to atone for the sins of the people.

Consider the irony and significance of the angelic announcement to these shepherds.

- God was announcing the birth of the final sacrificial Lamb to men who were watching over sacrificial lambs.

- God was announcing to men considered perpetually sinful that the Lamb had been born whose blood would cleanse their sins forever.

- God was announcing to men out of fellowship with the worship system of Israel that a baby had been born who could bring them into fellowship with God.

- God was announcing the gospel to men who were outcasts, assuring them that they could become members of God's family.

What a display of the wonderful, deep, grace of God!

UNIQUE MESSAGE

And an angel of the Lord suddenly stood before them, and the glory of the Lord shone around them; and they were terribly frightened. But the angel said to them, "Do not be afraid; for behold, I bring you good news of great joy which will be for all the people; for today in the city of David there has been born for you a Savior, who is Christ the Lord. This will be a sign for you: you will find a baby wrapped in cloths and lying in a manger."

And suddenly there appeared with the angel a multitude of the heavenly host praising God and saying, "Glory to God in the highest, and on earth peace among men with whom He is pleased." (Luke 2:9-14)

As the shepherds were watching their sheep, **an angel of the Lord suddenly stood before them**. When the New Testament opened, angels had not been seen by anybody on earth in more than four hundred years. Then, suddenly, angels are showing up everywhere. The angel Gabriel came to Zacharias (Luke 1:19). Then Gabriel came to Mary (Luke 1:26). And now an angel stood before the shepherds.

Gabriel appears to be one of God's chief messengers to humans. It was Gabriel who spoke to Daniel in Daniel 8:16 and again in Daniel 9:21. So it seems likely Gabriel was the one who now came to the shepherds with this announcement.

Luke 2:9 says **the glory of the Lord shone around them; and they were terribly frightened**. The **glory of the Lord** refers to the shekinah glory, the light of God's presence. For centuries God's glory had not shown anywhere. It had departed from the holy of holies and the temple because of the people's disobedience and rebellion (Ezekiel 10-11). Now, with the appearance of the angel, the Lord's glory engulfed the shepherds. Understandably, they were **terribly frightened**.

In verses 10-11 the angel told the shepherds,

"Do not be afraid; for behold, I bring you good news of great joy which will be for all the people; for today in the city of David there has been born for you a Savior, who is Christ the Lord."

Did you catch those words, **for you?** The One born in Bethlehem, **the city of David**, wasn't just born; He was born for you! Let me encourage you to write your name in the margin of your Bible beside those words in verse 11 as I have done, so that I can read it, **Today in the city of David there has been born for** *Stephen* **a Savior, who is Christ the Lord.**

In Luke 2:11 the angel used three titles to describe the baby Boy born that day in Bethlehem.

The first title is **Savior** (*sotēr*). This was a politically combustible term that was known throughout the Roman Empire. It was a title taken by the emperor Caesar Augustus, who was proclaimed in inscriptions to be the *savior* of the world.

Gentiles especially would perk up their ears at this title, and Jews, of course, would recognize it from their Scriptures, as well as from Roman culture.

The second title is **Christ** (*christos*). *Christos* means "anointed one." This title would have immediately arrested the attention of the Jews, for it was the title specifically designated for the messianic office. Only the Messiah could claim the title of Christ.

The last title summarizes it all in one breathtaking claim. The One born in Bethlehem that day was **Lord** (*kurios*). *Ku-*

rios is the Greek counterpart to the Hebrew term *Yahweh*. In fact, throughout the Greek translation of the Old Testament (Septuagint), more than six thousand times, *Yahweh* is translated *kurios*. **Lord** means God.

In one brief sentence, the angel revealed some astonishing truths.

We could read this announcement this way: "Today, in the city of David, there has been born for you a Savior, the anointed Messiah who is none other than God in the flesh."

Jesus is Savior, Messiah, and God. The true gospel demands that we acknowledge Him as all three.

The apostle Paul declared in Romans 10:9 that in order to be saved, you must confess with your mouth that Jesus is Lord. Jesus is the visible expression of deity. One day, when we look into the face of Jesus, we will indeed be looking into the face of God.

And with that announcement, this scene goes into surround sound:

And suddenly there appeared with the angel a multitude of the heavenly host praising God and saying… (Luke 2:13)

But weren't the angels singing? This verse says the heavenly host was **praising God and** *saying*. The original word translated **praising** here is *aineō*. This verb is rarely used in the Greek New Testament. However, it appears often in the Greek translation of the Old Testament for the verb *hallel*. That Hebrew verb means to praise, primarily through singing. Thus, *aineō* is interchangeable with *hallel*. Both words typically refer to praising God through *song*.

Therefore, we could paraphrase verse 13 as follows:

> And suddenly there appeared with the angel a multitude of the heavenly host, praising God by singing these lyrics—Glory to God in the highest, and on earth peace among men with whom He is pleased.

What singing this must have been as the heavens exploded with the angels' song of praise.

Job 38 tells us that angels sang at the dawn of creation, as God the Son, the Logos, spoke the worlds into existence. The book of Revelation also tells us that the believers in heaven will sing to the Lamb and the angels will join them.

So here, at this significant moment in world history, the angelic hosts burst forth with song.

UNDISTINGUISHED WITNESSES

When the angels had gone away from them into heaven, the shepherds began saying to one another, "Let us go straight to Bethlehem then, and see this thing that has happened which the Lord has made known to us." So they came in a hurry and found their way to Mary and Joseph, and the baby as He lay in the manger. (Luke 2:15-16)

The verb translated **found their way** means "discover after searching." There may have been several babies born that day in Bethlehem, but in verse 12 the angel gave the shepherds a sign that would help them identify the One they were searching for. The Messiah would be wrapped in cloths, lying in a feeding trough. That would have been unique!

When they had seen this, they made known the statement which had been told them about this Child. And all who heard it wondered at the things which were told them by the shepherds. But Mary treasured all these things, pondering them in her heart. The shepherds went back, glorifying and praising God for all that they had heard and seen, just as had been told them. (Luke 2:17-20)

It is interesting to see that now the shepherds were glorifying and praising God, which is exactly what the angels were doing earlier. The implication is that the shepherds were singing the song they'd just learned from the angels.

Has it ever occurred to you that angels haven't sung about the gospel and the grace of God on earth since the time of Jesus' birth?

God could send more angels to proclaim His message, couldn't He? So, why doesn't He? Why doesn't He write the message of His Son's preexistent deity in the clouds? Why doesn't He shake the earth with the chanting of millions of angels?

He could, but He has chosen from Luke 2 to this very day—and until His coming kingdom—to use ordinary, simple, undistinguished, sinful, faltering but forgiven members of His family to spread the word. God has chosen to use you and me, the redeemed, as His singers now.

It is our privilege and responsibility to make the announcement. We are now the witnesses to the truth of who Jesus really is. And just who is He?

- **The Savior** – capable of saving us from sin and death

- **The Christ** – capable of leading us to a heavenly home, free from sin and death

- **The Lord** – eternal God, capable of breaking the power of sin and death . . . forever.

Today, in the city of David, there has been born for you a Savior, who is Christ, the Lord.

Chapter 7

The Presentation of the Lamb

Luke 2:21-32

If asked what happened to Joseph, Mary, and Jesus after the shepherds left the manger scene in Bethlehem, the average Christian today would probably answer, "I'm not sure."

That's because the normal Christmas play ends somewhere around verse 20 of Luke chapter 2, which reads,

> The shepherds went back, glorifying and praising God for all they had heard and seen, just as had been told them.

For most Christians, that ends the significant scenes in the early days of Jesus, Joseph, and Mary.

Part of the challenge we face is that God the Father didn't disclose very much about the life of God the Son between His birth and His public ministry, which commenced at about the age of thirty. He knew that the incarnation would forever remain a mystery to us—and it was enough for us to contemplate God as a baby without His adding a lot of details about His childhood. So, for the most part, the record of Scripture is silent on those years.

Sadly, the Roman church attempted to lend a hand in the third and fourth centuries with a number of apocryphal books "filling in the gap" in Jesus' life. They did much damage.

Apocryphal means "hidden." The term came to refer to dubious or spurious writings by supposed church scholars who did nothing more than catalogue legends and myths that bolstered the growing church traditions regarding non-biblical subjects such as the role of Mary in redemption.

One particular apocryphal book, the Infancy Gospel of Thomas, attempts to fill in the gaps in the boyhood of Jesus but ends up portraying Him as being as selfish and sinful as any other child in need of redemption. It describes a young Jesus fashioning little sparrows out of mud one Sabbath day—an act that would have been considered working on the Sabbath and therefore forbidden. Some other children ran to tell on Jesus, but just as Joseph arrived to punish Jesus for profaning the Sabbath, Jesus breathed on the mud sparrows, and they came to life and flew away, leaving no evidence of His violation of the Sabbath. Pretty clever boy.

The Infancy Gospel of Thomas describes another occasion when a boy from the village threw a rock at young Jesus, hitting Him on the shoulder. Jesus turned around and cursed him, which caused the boy to immediately fall down dead.

In a similar episode, Jesus was playing in the rain one day, making little puddles of water that He miraculously made pure and drinkable. One boy came over and stomped all over the little puddles so the water drained away. Jesus told the boy he wouldn't live to see the next day, and the boy fell down dead.

The truth is, if I were Jesus, I would have done that. I can remember some kids in my neighborhood, and one bully in particular, that I would have toasted if I'd had the power.

We can imagine a child who has supernatural power doing the things this apocryphal work attributes to the young Jesus. But to attribute them to Jesus is to impose on Him our own sinful flesh.

Jesus also did some good things according to the Infancy Gospel of Thomas. It records that when Jesus was eight years old, He was helping Joseph cut wood for a bed frame. Joseph cut one of the boards two short, a costly mistake for this poor carpenter. But Jesus told Joseph to pull on one end of the board while He pulled on the other end, and the board miraculously stretched out to the perfect length.[1]

The trouble with these uninspired, apocryphal writings—and there are many of them—is that they describe a different Jesus. He becomes a rude, unkind, vengeful, self-centered, rebellious boy who uses His powers, not only to fix problems that make life difficult, but also to get rid of neighborhood children who offend Him.

The record of Scripture is vastly different. The Bible records that Jesus lived a life we can hardly imagine—a life of restraint and without sin. He did not use His powers to better Himself or cut down His enemies. He never sinned (Hebrews 4:15); He perfectly fulfilled the law (Matthew 5:17). In doing so, He qualified as the unblemished Lamb, sacrificed for the sins of the whole world (1 John 2:2).

So, let's go back to Scripture alone and ask what the divinely inspired Bible reveals about the childhood of Jesus.

The Bible is not as silent as the average Christmas play might lead you to believe. It wasn't over after the shepherds left the manger scene. It was just *beginning*. In fact, eight days after the manger scene, some wonderful events began to unfold in the life of the infant Messiah.

Beginning with Luke 2:21, we see Jesus and His parents involved in three ceremonies that reveal a lot about Joseph and Mary's faith in God and submission to His will.

THE CEREMONY OF IDENTIFICATION

And when eight days had passed, before His circumcision, His name was then called Jesus, the name given by the angel before He was conceived in the womb. (Luke 2:21)

Eight days after birth, every Jewish baby boy would be circumcised—that is, if the baby's parents cared at all about God's commands. Circumcision brought the boy into the national life of the Hebrew people and identified him with Abraham's household.

The practice was commanded in Genesis 17 for all Abraham's descendants as a sign of the covenant God made with the patriarch. So, had Jesus not been circumcised, He would not have been identified with His people even though both Joseph and Mary were descendants of Abraham.

This act was a statement of Joseph and Mary's faith. They were following God's Word and identifying Jesus with the Abrahamic covenant. Because they fulfilled this command, Jesus Christ was eligible to fulfill the promises God had pledged to Abraham.[2]

For every faithful Jewish family, circumcision was considered so sacred a duty that it could be carried out on the Sabbath day. A Jewish leader or doctor would perform the simple procedure, and during this ceremony the parents would announce the name of the child.

The pain-filled cry of Jesus, the Son of God, pierced the air as He experienced His first moment of suffering at the hand of mankind. These tears were among His first upon taking on human flesh. His humiliation and suffering had already begun.

Joseph and Mary were also suffering, being ostracized, confused, and alone. These two—Mary probably not more than a teenager—had traveled to Bethlehem under a cloud of suspicion . . . and all because of the will of God.

It had been a whirlwind. Their lives had been upended. It had already taken an angel to convince Joseph to take Mary to be his wife after she was found to be pregnant during their betrothal.

This must have been the scandal of Joseph's family and their entire village. There was no wedding ceremony or wedding march. There was no family festival in which the village celebrated the union of Joseph and Mary.

The birth of Mary's Child would only add an exclamation point to their apparent guilt. Joseph and Mary would never live this down. The rumors would never go away.

At some point Joseph and Mary moved from the stable into humble quarters somewhere in Bethlehem. Joseph probably took odd jobs to eke out their existence.

Even though they would never be viewed by the Jewish community as credible, godly, obedient children of Abraham, they were still determined to identify their Son with the Jewish family through circumcision. They refused to acquiesce to public perception.

Note how carefully they identified Jesus with the law of God, and ask yourself what it takes to keep you from submitting to the Word of God. Is a false accusation enough to thwart your obedience to the Lord? How about rumors, criticism, pain, gossip, failure, or abandonment? Such things did not deter Joseph and Mary from following God's instructions.

Do you ever find yourself saying, "If doing the right thing causes so much discomfort, surely God will understand if I wiggle out of this one"? It was against the backdrop of *permanent* discomfort that Joseph and Mary determined not to miss one step of obedience.

On the eighth day, they brought forward their little Boy and thus sent forth a message: "Even though everyone believes this Child is illegitimate, the result of fornication, this family and this Boy will identify with the people of God and the Word of God and the will of God.

It was at this ceremony that **His name was then called Jesus**. This was the name chosen for Him before time began. The angel had come to both Mary and Joseph individually to tell them that when the ceremony of identification came, they were to give Him the name Jesus (Matt. 1:21; Luke 1:31).

To understand the significance of this name, we have to travel back to the first person in recorded history to be given this name.

He had been born into Egyptian slavery along with all the other Hebrew slaves under Pharaoh's cruel reign. This little boy was given his original name as a sheer act of faith. He was named Hoshea, which means "salvation."

G. Campbell Morgan wrote that this name was a sigh and a hope—a sob from his parents who dared by faith to believe in deliverance so much that they named their son Salvation.[3]

He would eventually grow up to become the assistant to Moses, and Moses would change his name (Numbers 13:16). Moses simply took letters out of the Lord's great name Yahweh, or Jehovah, and some letters out of the name of the boy, Hoshea, and wove them into one name so that the young man became Yehoshua, meaning "Jehovah is salvation."

The name was shortened to Joshua. The Greek counterpart to this Hebrew name was Yeshua, or Jesus. It carried the idea that the person so named would be the agent of salvation; he would be the deliverer.

Hundreds of little boys named Jesus were playing in the streets and villages throughout Israel when Mary's Son was born. They were named by fathers and mothers perhaps with the vague notion that their sons would play a role in the deliverance of Israel.

This little Boy born in Bethlehem would, for He is both Jehovah and salvation.

Did the rabbi or others present at the ceremony shake their heads at the audacity of this peasant couple giving their

Son such a name? Did Joseph and Mary actually believe their Child, who from all appearances was conceived in sin, could ever deliver anybody?

Following this ceremony, Joseph and Mary and their eight-day-old Son went back to their undisclosed home in Bethlehem. They had carefully met the demands of the law.

THE CEREMONY OF REDEMPTION

And when the days for their purification according to the law of Moses were completed, they brought Him up to Jerusalem to present Him to the Lord (as it is written in the Law of the Lord, "Every firstborn male that opens the womb shall be called holy to the Lord"). (Luke 2:22-23)

In going to Jerusalem for the purification of the mother after giving birth, Joseph and Mary were following what was set forth in Leviticus 12. There the days of purification for the mother of a male child was stated as being forty days. After seven days the ceremony of identification (circumcision) was to be observed. Then after waiting another thirty-three days, she was to go to a priest and offer a sacrifice. She would then be declared clean.

So, forty days after Jesus' birth, Mary and Joseph went to Jerusalem for this ceremony, which is described in verse 24. However, they took advantage of this time in the city to fulfill another requirement of the law first.

Verse 23 mentions that according to the law, **every first-born male that opens the womb shall be called holy to the Lord.**

God had a special claim on the firstborn males. They were to be holy, which means "separated unto God." This goes back to Exodus 13, where God's special ownership of the firstborn is connected to the preservation of Israel's first-born through the final plague on Egypt.

The parents of a firstborn son had to pay five shekels to redeem their son from priestly service (Numbers 18:14-16). Thus, they effectively bought their son back from God.

If the male child was from the tribe of Levi, he would serve in a priestly role in the theocracy. The priests were the government; they were the senators and representatives. They ran the religious and civil system, or at least as much as the Roman government allowed them during the days of Christ.[4]

However, since Christ was born into the tribe of Judah, He was not required to serve in the priestly system. There-fore, Joseph and Mary were able to pay the redemption tax and redeem Jesus back from God. This practice was called the redemption of the firstborn.[5]

They probably didn't grasp the irony of this redemption. They were purchasing Jesus back from God, when Jesus had come to purchase a people for God. They were essentially redeeming the Redeemer.

Note, however, that obeying the law only added to Joseph and Mary's poverty. They had already paid the census tax in Bethlehem, and now they paid five shekels, which amounted to several weeks' wages, in order to once again fulfill the letter of the law.

The will of God was taxing, tiring, uncomfortable, uneasy, lonely, and expensive. They were God's chosen couple to bear and raise the Redeemer. But so far, God had not paid them anything but a few angelic visits, and they seemed to be paying for everything else!

To Joseph and Mary, however, cost was never the issue—obedience was. And they were willing to meet and pay any price obedience demanded.

In fact, they were not required by law to physically bring Jesus to Jerusalem for the redemption of the firstborn. They could have simply paid the five shekels to a local priest.

They went above and beyond what was required. They wanted to go to Jerusalem and to the temple itself to present Jesus to the priest and pay the redemption tax. Why? Because they realized that even though they were redeeming Jesus from priestly service, they were also presenting Him **to the Lord** as the last phrase of verse 22 tells us.

No one else knew who Jesus was, but they did. And they knew God did.

Notice the irony here:

- They dedicated God the Son to God the Father.

- They presented the Lamb of God to God.

- They brought the Lord of the temple to the temple of the Lord.[6]

- They brought the Object of true worship to the house of worship.

- They brought into the court of women the One who would rip down the curtain between mankind and the holy of holies.

Into all the hubbub in the temple that day they brought their Child. Every ritual, every sacrifice, and every activity on those temple grounds illustrated, pointed toward, and anticipated the coming final sacrifice. And those present had no idea that the Lamb who would be the final sacrifice was among them.

Hundreds of people were milling around, prayers were being prayed, incense was being burned, and sacrifices were being made, and there *He* was. Unknown to almost all those people, the Messiah, the Deliverer, their Salvation had arrived.

THE CEREMONY OF PURIFICATION

And to offer a sacrifice according to what was said in the Law of the Lord, "A PAIR OF TURTLE-DOVES OR TWO YOUNG PIGEONS." (Luke 2:24)

There was still one more ceremony required by the law, and they had come to Jerusalem to observe it. According to the law, Mary was ceremonially unclean following the birth of Jesus. After forty days she was required to bring a pair of sacrifices to the priest so that she could be declared clean. One sacrifice atoned for the defilement of delivering a child and issuing blood. The second sacrifice restored her communion with God and allowed her to participate in the temple worship.

The idea that Mary had no need for atonement and she was received into heaven after living a life without sin is simply not in the Bible. She *was* in need of atonement. She *was* in need of a sacrifice for her uncleanness.

So here we see her bringing sacrifices, not for Jesus, not for Joseph, but for herself. Bringing the perfect, sinless Son of God into the world did not make her sinless; it defiled her in a religious, ceremonial sense just as it did for any other woman who bore a child. She was not exempted from the law. In fact, she was impure and could not worship or go near the temple until the forty days were completed.

According to the law, Mary was to bring to the priest at the temple a lamb for a burnt offering and a pigeon or turtledove for a sin offering. If she and her husband didn't have the money for a lamb, she was allowed to bring two pigeons or two turtledoves (Lev. 12:6-8). Turtledoves and pigeons were the only birds allowed by the law as sacrificial gifts.[7]

Lambs were much more expensive than pigeons. Turtledoves migrated and were harder to find; but just like today, pigeons were everywhere. The fact that Mary and Joseph brought birds instead of a lamb indicates their poverty.

Mary would have been ushered over to the gate nearest the sanctuary just beyond the court of women. She then would have presented her two birds and watched from a distance as the smoke of her offering ascended to God.

Imagine, as Mary stood there watching her sacrifice offered to God, she held in her arms the final Sacrifice. She couldn't afford to buy a lamb to give to the priest for an offering, but she had delivered into the world *the* Lamb for the final offering.

Mary and Joseph carefully did all the law required and even more. And with that they were finished. They might have quietly slipped away and left unnoticed had God not prepared two witnesses to be on hand to testify that the Messiah had come.

THE CONFIRMATION OF WITNESSES

And there was a man in Jerusalem whose name was Simeon; and this man was righteous and devout, looking for the consolation of Israel; and the Holy Spirit was upon him. And it had been revealed to him by the Holy Spirit that he would not see death before he had seen the Lord's Christ. (Luke 2:25-26)

Luke tells us in verse 25 that Simeon was a **righteous and devout** man, who was **looking for the consolation of Israel**. **Consolation** means "comfort" and refers here to the comfort the Messiah would bring to the nation.

Some have suggested that Simeon was the son of the famous rabbi Hillel and the father of Gamaliel, the apostle Paul's tutor (Acts 22:3). If so, this was the Simeon who became the leading member of the Sanhedrin in AD 13. It is intriguing that the Mishnah, the commentary on Jewish life and process, relates the stories and accomplishments of all the great rabbis but ignores Simeon. Could this be because this man believed in Jesus Christ and would have been an embarrassment to its Jewish writers?[8]

Simeon's name means "hearing," and clearly he was listening. In fact, verse 26 informs us that the Spirit of God had promised him he would not die until he had seen the Messiah.

We can imagine that perhaps for years Simeon came to the temple looking at all the babies, longing to see the Messiah.

There's no telling how many young couples he met and then turned away, inwardly disappointed.

But he was not disappointed when he met Joseph and Mary. The Spirit of God identified the Child they brought into the temple as the long-awaited Messiah.

And he came in the Spirit into the temple; and when the parents brought in the child Jesus, to carry out for Him the custom of the Law, then he took Him in his arms, and blessed God. (Luke 2:27-28)

Simeon knew *this* Baby was the One.

A little later an elderly prophetess named Anna who was in the temple that day confirmed that the Child Jesus was indeed Israel's Messiah. She publicly gave thanks to God and began to tell everyone on the temple grounds who was also looking for the Redeemer that He had arrived (Luke 2:36-38).

What incredible joy! And what a commotion there must have been throughout the temple area.

There stood Simeon, holding the Infant Jesus. As he did so, he began to speak:

> **Now Lord, You are releasing Your bond-servant to depart in peace, according to Your word; for my eyes have seen Your salvation, which You have prepared in the presence of all peoples, A LIGHT OF REVELATION TO THE GENTILES, and the glory of Your people Israel.** (Luke 2:29-32)

In other words, "I've seen salvation with my own eyes. I've seen the Savior, and now I can die in peace."

In Simeon's words there is truth for all of us. We are not ready to die until by faith we have seen the Savior, until we have embraced Him and His truth in our hearts.

You are not ready to encounter the shadow of death unless you have seen the Light of the World.

Joseph, Mary, and presumably Anna and scores of curious people watched and listened as Simeon, holding the Baby in his arms, no doubt with tears in his eyes, announced the identity of Jesus.

The priests went about their duties, and the people continued bringing their sacrifices. But there, in the midst of it all, was the Lamb. God had taken on human flesh so He could die as the final sacrifice for sin and redeem His people forever.

The songwriter wrote of the newborn Messiah with these words:

Hope has hands, freedom has feet
Truth will stand, the Word will speak
The holy and lowly will finally embrace
For love has a heartbeat, and grace has a face.

Compassion has a tear, joy has a laughter
And here ever after peace has a smile
Redemption's blood has veins to flow in
A temple to glow in, Light is a child.[9]

Grace has a face!

Chapter 8

The King-Makers

Matthew 2:1-12

There are well-meaning believers who think we shouldn't celebrate Christmas at all, given the pagan origins of many of the traditions related to Christmas.

There is no denying that the Romans decorated their temples and pagan altars with greenery and candles. And when the Romans conquered the British Isles, they found Druids who were using mistletoe in their pagan worship ceremonies, along with holly and ivy for decor.

By the fifth century, all these trappings had become part of the church's celebration of Christmas.

The Puritans reacted against this and tried to stamp out any observance of Christmas. They passed a law in England in 1644 that made Christmas Day an official working day. For a while in England, it was illegal to cook special desserts like plum pudding and mince pie in December. The Puritans deliberately worked on December 25 to show their disdain for such observances.[1]

If you decide not to observe something because it has worldly associations or even origins—and you want to follow this approach consistently—you will need to carefully study history and ancient civilizations.

You won't want to refer to the first month as January because that would be associating your schedule with the name of the Roman god with two faces: one in front, looking ahead to the new year, and one face in back, reflecting on the old year that has just passed. And you won't drive a car or truck manufactured by Mazda since that company's name came from the conquering god of the ancient Persians.

While you're at it, you might as well take the fish symbol off your bumper. That symbol was in use long before early Christians adapted it to their own purpose. The fish was associated with several pagan goddesses before Christians borrowed it and used it to mark their meeting places. Because the symbol was so common, nobody took any notice.

The point is, if you don't want any correlation to pagan icons or symbols of ancient ungodly practices, you might want to move to a remote cave. But then again, living in a cave to escape evil has pagan origins too.

The Apostle Paul gave us a helpful guideline in Romans 14:5-6:

> One person regards one day above another, another regards every day alike. Each person must be fully convinced in his own mind. He who observes the day, observes it for the Lord.

In other words, no day is any more special than another. But if you choose to make one day or one season special, make the most of it for the glory of God—and give it redemptive meaning.

This is what Martin Luther did. Many believe he was the first to come up with the idea of taking lighted globes and attaching them to a Christmas tree, signifying the birth of the Light of the World. He took something pagan and gave it redemptive purpose.

The fact that we observe Christmas is not the issue. *How* we observe it and *why* we observe it is.

Christmastime is a fantastic opportunity for us to exalt Jesus Christ in our community, and we should take full advantage of it.

Let's make sure the message is clear so that people know why we celebrate and why they should too. Christmas is more than symbols, and that demands that we separate the myths from the message.

In the Gospel of Matthew we find some of the most mythologized participants in the usual Christmas play: the wise men, or magi.

THE ARRIVAL OF THE MAGI

Now after Jesus was born in Bethlehem of Judea in the days of Herod the king, magi from the east arrived in Jerusalem, saying, "Where is He who has been born King of the Jews? For we saw His star in the east and have come to worship Him." (Matthew 2:1-2)

Matthew places Jesus' birth **in Bethlehem of Judea in the days of Herod the king**, as does Luke (2:1-7). Some time after His birth, **magi from the east arrived in Jerusalem.**

Magi comes from the Greek word *magoi* and gives us our words *magic*, *magician*, and *magistrate*.

This verse tells us these men were **from the east**. Literally, translated, it says they came from "the rising," a reference to the rising of the sun. They were from the kingdom of the Medes and Persians.

Herodotus, the ancient Greek historian, informs us the magi were a special caste of men, highly trained in the arts and sciences. They were the high priests, university professors, and political power brokers all rolled into one.

The magi were practitioners of Zoroastrianism, the religion of Persia at the time Jesus was born. The principle element in Zoroastrians' worship was fire. They had an altar with fire they kept burning, believing it had originally been given to them from heaven. They practiced animal sacrifice and believed in only one god, whose name was Mazda.

Historians also tell us that no Persian was ever able to become king without mastering the scientific and religious disciplines of the magi. Only then was the heir to the throne approved and crowned by magi.[2]

Matthew doesn't tell us how many magi arrived. Early church tradition said there were twelve, but during the Middle Ages, the number was reduced to three. They were given names—Caspar, Melchior, and Balthasar—and said to be representatives of the three sons of Noah. Supposedly their skulls were miraculously preserved and discovered in the twelfth century by the bishop of Cologne. The great cathedral of Cologne still exhibits these skulls, encased in a jewel-studded glass encasement.

Such myths offer no serious answers to the questions raised by the narrative of Scripture, and there *are* significant questions.

Why make a trip across the continent, in a journey that took a year? What would make the magi assume that when they arrived in Jerusalem, people would automatically know where the Messiah was living? Why would they be willing to slip in the front door of Israel and slip out the back door into oblivion?[3]

And most importantly, why would they even be interested in a Jewish Messiah?

To find answers to these questions, we must go back several centuries before Jesus' birth to the time when Jews were taken captive by the Babylonian kingdom to the east.

Among the deported Jews were several teenagers who were handed over to the magi to be trained in the university. Among them are some familiar names: Daniel, Shadrach, Meshach, and Abednego. Daniel had such a profound effect on King Nebuchadnezzar that the king promoted him to be the chief leader over all the magi in the kingdom of Babylon (Daniel 2:48).

Later in life, Daniel had earned such respect and power that when the Persians conquered Babylon, they retained Daniel in a leadership position. You may remember that other Persian politicians plotted to have Daniel thrown to the lions. The magi were *not* a part of that plot. They evidently had tremendous respect for Daniel.

Remarkably, seventy years of godly influence by the life and testimony of Daniel brought two kings to an acknowledgment of, if not faith in, Daniel's God. Apparently, Daniel had a similar impact on many of the magi as well.

But how would the magi in Matthew 2, who lived hundreds of years after Daniel, be prompted by a star to come in search of the Messiah, the **King of the Jews?** What did they mean when they announced to Herod, **For we saw His star in the east and have come to worship Him?**

First, this text reveals that the magi who traveled to Jerusalem were already believers. They were ready to worship the Savior. They already believed the Scriptures. They knew the Messiah had been born. The One they had come to worship was the **King of the Jews,** and it's clear they equated this title with Israel's Messiah, or Christ. Herod understood this too, for he responded by gathering the religious leaders and asking them where the Messiah was to be born (verse 4).

These magi, descendants of Daniel's converts, no doubt arrived in a large caravan. With them would have been servants to cook and to keep the herds they needed for food during the long journey, as well as a large division of soldiers to protect them as they traveled through foreign kingdoms. These soldiers also would have protected the costly gifts the magi had with them.

The magi were Persian dignitaries who were renowned for their power and privilege. And they stood in a long line of Gentile believers that stretched back to Daniel, their leading wise man.

There's still the question of why an astral sign would prompt their journey. How would they have connected a star with the Messiah?

Daniel evidently had at his disposal the Torah, the Law of Moses, and the writings of some of the prophets. Apparently he and other godly Jews living in captivity had faithfully taught the magi of the coming Messiah.

Listen to one verse we could imagine Daniel explaining to his magi friends:

> The oracle of him who hears the words of God, and knows the knowledge of the Most High, who sees the vision of the Almighty . . . I see him, but not now; I behold him, but not near; a star shall come forth from Jacob, and a scepter shall rise from Israel. (Numbers 24:16-17)

In this Old Testament passage, the Messiah is called a star.

Daniel evidently taught them from Isaiah's prophecy, which says:

> Arise, shine; for your light has come, and the glory of the Lord has risen upon you. . . . the Lord will rise upon you and His glory will appear upon you. Nations will come to your light, and kings to the brightness of your rising. (Isaiah 60:1-3)

Here we see the same idea of a star rising in brightness, and it is associated with the Lord, the Messiah.

Similarly, in Revelation 22:16, Jesus Christ is referred to as "the bright morning star."

We must understand, however, that the magi didn't see just any star. This wasn't some meteor, or comet, or alignment of the planets. This was a messianic *sign*. It was star-like, but it was, in fact, the light of God's presence—His shekinah glory.

The Greek word for star (*aster*) can be understood to mean "brilliance" or "radiance."

- This was the light that guided the people of Israel as they journeyed through the wilderness (Exodus 13:21).

- This was the consuming fire on the mountaintop (Exodus 24:17).

- This was the light that made the face of Moses glow after he had met with God (Exodus 34:30).

- This was the glory of God in radiant light the shepherds saw around the angels (Luke 2:9).

- This was the heavenly brilliance of the resurrected Christ that knocked Saul of Tarsus to the ground and blinded him (Acts 9:3).

- This was the vision of John the apostle as he saw the light of Christ's face shining like the sun (Revelation 1:16).

This was the same light that appeared to these Persian magi and led them to embark on their journey to Jerusalem.

How do we explain that it seemed to disappear when they arrived in Jerusalem? How do we explain that it suddenly seemed to reappear when they left Herod's palace? How do we explain the star literally standing over *the very house* where the Child was staying?

There is only one way to explain it all. They were being led by the light of God's glory—and it seems that they were the only ones who saw it.

What was so important about these Persian magi coming to give Christ gifts? As one author suggested, this revealed that the birth of Jesus had worldwide impact and influence. It also showed that the Messiah was coming through Israel as a gift from God to all nations, not just to the Jews.[4]

THE APPREHENSION OF HEROD

When Herod the king heard this, he was troubled, and all Jerusalem with him. (Matthew 2:3)

Herod must have been biting his tongue to keep from saying what he *really* wanted to say.

This was Herod the Great! He had been appointed by his father to rule the province of Galilee. And his father had been appointed by none other than Julius Caesar to rule Judea. Herod eventually extended his rule over Judea after his father's death.

By the time we meet Herod in Matthew 2, he was seventy years old and insanely jealous of his power and his throne.

One of Herod's ten wives, Miriamne, had a brother, Aristobulus, who was the Jewish high priest. Herod became so fearful of the popularity of Aristobulus that he had him drowned, after which he financed a huge funeral where he pretended to weep. Then Herod killed Miriamne and her mother.

In his final two years of life, his paranoia became so great that he murdered his two oldest sons. Five days before his death, he ordered the execution of his next eldest son, determined that he would have no rival to his throne.

One of the last things Herod did before he died was imprison many distinguished Jews on trumped-up charges. He gave the order that these men and women were to be executed the very moment he died in order to ensure that there would be weeping in Jerusalem. Even if people weren't weeping for him, the days following his death would be filled with mourning.

This man was a cold-hearted, vain, corrupt, paranoid killer. He also bore an important title. As an older man who had gained the favor of the Roman emperor, he was granted his wish by the Roman senate, who gave him the title "King of the Jews." *He* was the King of the Jews. That was *his* title and *his* throne!

It was during these last two years, when Herod was eliminating every threat to his throne, that this entourage of Persian dignitaries appeared in Jerusalem, asking, **Where is He who has been born King of the Jews?** Notice that they were not looking for one who *would be* born but One who *had been* born.

And to this newborn One they gave a shocking title: **King of the Jews!** Of all they could have said, nothing could have been more upsetting to Herod than those words: **King of the Jews.**

Matthew tells us that **when Herod the king heard this, he was troubled**. The word means "visibly shaken."

The magi were known as king-makers, and Herod knew that as well. In fact, all of Jerusalem knew it, and they were just as troubled, although for different reasons. Someone had dared to take Herod's throne and title, and that was enough to trouble everyone.

Our world is filled with Herods. Few are going around murdering people, of course, but there are many who insist on the right to be king. They alone will inhabit the throne room of their own life and heart.

In their minds, nobody has the right to interfere with their career, their position, their power, their ambition, their plans, their lifestyle. They are not about to let anybody else be king of their lives.[5]

Reveal to people that Jesus Christ deserves to be their master and king, and watch as they become *visibly shaken*. Tell them they must bow and surrender to Christ's reign, and watch as they burn with anger and bite their tongue to keep from saying what they are thinking— "I don't need saving. I alone am king. I am the master of my fate!"

Don't misunderstand; they are okay with a little Christmas caroling once a year, but they want Christ left in the manger—or on the cross. Our religious world takes only brief note of Him at His birth or at His death.

Such people don't want to hear about the sovereign, ascended Lord. They don't want to talk about surrendered priorities and plans and morals and lifestyles. That would ruin their Christmas spirit!

Herod wanted nothing of that either, but He had just been confronted with his worst nightmare. Somebody else was laying claim to the title, "King of the Jews." And it wasn't just anybody who had delivered the news.

THE APATHY OF THE JEWISH LEADERS

Gathering together all the chief priests and scribes of the people, he inquired of them where the Messiah was to be born. They said to him, "In Bethlehem of Judea; for this is what has been written by the prophet: 'AND YOU, BETHLETHEM, LAND OF JUDAH, ARE BY NO MEANDS LEAST AMONG THE LEADERS OF JUDAH; FOR OUT OF YOU SHALL COME FORTH A RULER WHO WILL SHEPHERD MY PEOPLE ISRAEL." (Matthew 2:4-6)

Herod understood immediately that the wise men were referring to Israel's Messiah, and he inquired of the Jewish scholars concerning the birthplace of the prophesied Deliverer. They answered him by quoting Micah 5:2, a prophecy they had evidently memorized. They knew the Messiah was going to be born in Bethlehem.

Shockingly, the Jewish leaders who told Herod where the Messiah was to be born didn't care enough to walk the five miles from Jerusalem to Bethlehem to check it out. You'd think some of them would have immediately run down there to either confirm or dispel as rumors what the magi were spreading around Jerusalem.

These men knew the Scriptures, but they missed the Savior.

The wise men, on the other hand, traveled for many months over a great distance to find the newborn Jewish King whom the star indicated had been born. Persia was located in modern-day Iran, so these men traveled through what is today Iran and Iraq and down into the land of Palestine. It was a journey of several thousand miles. Further, it would have taken them several weeks or even months to prepare for the journey once the star appeared.

THE APPEAL OF HEROD

Then Herod secretly called the magi and determined from them the exact time the star appeared. And he sent them to Bethlehem and said, "Go and search carefully for the Child; and when you have found Him, report to me, so that I too may come and worship Him."
(Matthew 2:7-8)

Learning that the Messiah was to be born in nearby Bethlehem allowed Herod to answer the magi's question about where He could be found. More important for Herod, it also allowed him to hatch a plot to eliminate the challenger to his throne. His intent was hardly to worship the Jewish Messiah but to determine His approximate age and exactly who He was so he could kill Him.

Herod's well-practiced ability to hide his true intentions served him well in his appeal to the magi. His words must have seemed reasonable and believable to them, for he was able to enlist the unsuspecting magi in his plan.

THE ADORATION OF JESUS CHRIST

After hearing the king, they went their way; and the star, which they had seen in the east, went on before them until it came and stood over the place where the Child was. When they saw the star, they rejoiced exceedingly with great joy. After coming into the house they saw the Child with Mary His mother; and they fell to the ground and worshiped Him. Then, opening their treasures, they presented to Him gifts of gold, frankincense, and myrrh. And having been warned by God in a dream not to return to Herod, the magi left for their own country by another way. (Matthew 2:9-12)

When the magi left Herod, they turned toward Bethlehem. At that point, they again saw the star they had seen at the outset of their long journey. This implies that it had originally appeared for a short time, alerting them to the Messiah's birth so that they traveled to Jerusalem. Now it reappeared to their great joy, reaffirming God's unique, shining guidance.

The appearance of the star was not merely to lead them to Bethlehem, which they now knew from the Jewish Scriptures was the prophesied birthplace, but to direct them to the specific place where the Child Messiah was to be found. It did this as it specifically **stood over the place where the Child was**.

Here the text dispels another of the Christmas myths. When the wise men arrived in Bethlehem, they did not arrive at the stable. Verse 11 says they came **into the house**. And there they **saw the Child**. The word here is *paidion*, the

116

Greek word for young child, not *brephos*, the word for baby, which is used in Luke 2:16.

By the time the magi had arrived, Jesus was anywhere from one to two years of age.

The magi entered the house and **fell** down before this young Child and **worshiped Him**. The expression indicates the magi fell to their knees with their heads to the ground and then, in the oriental fashion of their day, kissed his feet and even the ground near his feet.

We can imagine little Jesus, holding on to his mother's robe, wide-eyed, receiving worship from the king-makers of a Gentile empire.

What's more, these king-makers brought gifts. First, they gave Him **gold**. Seneca, the Roman philosopher and writer who lived during the days of Christ, said that in Persia no one would approach a king without a gift and gold was the proper gift for a king. The magi brought a gift for a king, the One who was heir to the throne of David.[6]

They also gave Him **frankincense**. This is a gummy substance from the Boswellia tree that was used by the priests in the Old Testament in their priestly service of intercession.[7]

They gave gold to the King and frankincense to the High Priest!

And then they gave Him the strangest of gifts—**myrrh**, a sweet, fragrant substance that came from a small thorn tree. Gum from the tree's sap was mixed with wine to form a narcotic, pain-dulling drink. This was the beverage offered to Christ on the cross, which He refused to drink (Mark 15:23).

Myrrh was also commonly used in wrapping a corpse as it was prepared for burial. It would be enfolded in the shroud to keep the linen strips in place and also serve as a perfume.

The magi gave myrrh to the One who would die and be wrapped with it in the tomb.

They gave Him three gifts: gold for the King of Kings, frankincense for the Great High Priest, and myrrh for the suffering Savior who would redeem people from among every nation on the earth.

Verse 12 informs us that the magi were warned in Bethlehem about the maniac in Jerusalem and told not to return to him. They returned to their country by a different route, avoiding Jerusalem. These wise men, thus, disappear from the pages of Scripture. Their mission was accomplished, as these Gentile dignitaries added their testimony to that of the humble Jewish shepherds and the elderly Simeon and Anna.

*****

In these few verses in Matthew 2, we see three responses of the world to the announcement of Christ's birth—the message of Christmas. From the first century to the twenty-first century, the world and cultures have changed, but the responses of mankind have not.

There are still those who *hate* Him, as Herod did; and there are those who *ignore* Him, as the religious leaders did. But, thank God, there are also those who *worship* Him today, as the magi did, acknowledging Him and praising Him as the Christ, the true and living Savior!

Chapter 9

Israel's Most Wanted

Matthew 2:13-23

At the height of World War II, as Adolph Hitler's bombers pummeled England, Winston Churchill could be heard on the radio, broadcasting his stubborn refusal to surrender. He continually encouraged the British people to fight on.

In a series of speeches, Churchill declared, "I have nothing to offer you but blood, toil, tears and sweat," and "We shall go on to the end. We shall fight in the seas and oceans, we shall fight with growing confidence in the air; we shall defend our island, whatever the cost may be; we shall never surrender."[1]

What would happen if we told people Christ has nothing to offer them but blood, toil, tears, and sweat?

Maybe it's time we re-advertized Christianity. Maybe it's time we witnessed to people and then told them that if they want to follow Christ, He demands that they carry a cross.

With the growing animosity of our culture toward the Christian church, Christians are becoming frightened and even angered that their convictions and freedoms are no longer being respected. But when did God say the world would be our friend? When did the church ever receive a promise that the world would respect our convictions? When did God ever assure us that luxury and freedom are our rights?

Sadly, the television is stocked with pseudo-pastors and pseudo-Bible teachers who continue to promote the lie that an easy path through this life is synonymous with the narrow way that leads to everlasting life. No wonder people today, especially in America, who decide to "give Jesus a try" are shocked when instead of getting a catalog from heaven with La-Z-Boys to choose from, they get a sword, shield, and helmet.

Jesus Christ said, "I will build My church; and the gates of Hades will not overpower it" (Matthew 16:18). That is a wonderful promise, but it also implies a continuing struggle—not just institutionally but personally. So, strap on your armor.

Even Jesus Christ, the perfect Man, the obedient Son, the sinless Savior, faced challenges. He suffered hunger, sleeplessness, temptation, abandonment, and misunderstanding. Who are we to demand anything less?

The shadow of the cross did not fall across Jesus' path only when He turned thirty. The conflict between heaven and hell and the blood, toil, tears, and sweat began much earlier in His earthly life. Indeed, the same chapter of Matthew's Gospel that recounts the arrival of the magi announcing the birth of the King also introduces the struggle that began immediately thereafter, engulfing not just Jesus but primarily Joseph and Mary.

The events recorded in the second half of Matthew 2 center around the fulfillment of three Old Testament prophecies.

ESCAPE INTO EGYPT

Now when they [the magi] **had gone, behold, an angel of the Lord appeared to Joseph in a dream and said, "Get up! Take the Child and His mother and flee to Egypt, and remain there until I tell you; for Herod is going to search for the Child to destroy Him." So Joseph got up and took the Child and His mother while it was still night, and left for Egypt. He remained there until the death of Herod. This was to ful- fill what had been spoken by the Lord through the prophet: "OUT OF EGYPT I CALLED MY SON."** (Matthew 2:13-15)

Apparently very shortly after the departure of the magi, an angel appeared to Joseph in a dream and told him to **get up.** Joseph was not to finish his rest. He was to get up in the middle of the night, get Mary and Jesus and run for their lives.

They were going to another country, where they would hide out until it was safe for them to return. There could be no delay.

This was an unexpected and hard path for Joseph and Mary.

If you take your family on an extended trip, you have to think through the packing process, the travel dates, and the schedule. You have to remember money, passports, and tick- ets and find someone to take care of things at home while you're gone. You choose the most convenient time to depart, and by the time you leave, you probably know where you'll be staying when you arrive.

For Joseph and Mary, there was no time for any of that—no map, no choice of departure time, no time to pack just the right things. In fact, the word **flee** in verse 13 is a translation of the Greek word *pheugo*, which means to seek safety in flight. It's the same word from which our English word *fugitive* is derived.[2]

In other words, Joseph, Mary, and Jesus were now fugitives on the run . . . they were now Israel's most wanted!

The angel told Joseph specifically where they were to run (**flee to Egypt**), how long they were to stay there (**remain their until I tell you**), and why all this was necessary (**Herod is going to search for the Child to destroy Him**).

The grammar in this text indicates that their flight was the beginning of an action that was to be continued. In other words, they were not to stop until they were safely within Egypt and beyond the reach of Herod. From Bethlehem to the border of Egypt was about seventy-five miles.[3]

Joseph was given no specific address, and he wasn't told anyone would be waiting for them when they arrived or where they would be staying. He was not even given directions for the safest route there. He was told simply to run—in the middle of the night!

God could have protected Joseph and his little family right under the vain nose of Herod. He could have deposed Herod and blinded the soldiers sent to find the newborn King. He could have miraculously hidden the family like a suitcase of smuggled Bibles. He could have, but He didn't.

God chose to protect them by the very ordinary and non-miraculous means of *flight*. The will of God meant hardship and suffering, but He would sustain them through it.

The message for Joseph and his family to run came supernaturally—the word of God arrived in a dream. The word of God has come to us in a supernatural Book. The Holy Spirit, through conformity to the Word, provokes our hearts and minds so that we take steps in obedience to Him. All our questions aren't answered, and neither were theirs. We walk by faith in God's word, as did Joseph and Mary. God did not do something for them that He withholds from us.

The medieval church couldn't imagine adversity being the will of God the Father for His Son, so apocryphal writings compiled legends and myths to make it seem less difficult for Joseph and Mary to obey.

One legend recorded that when Joseph, Mary, and Jesus needed a place to sleep one night, they sought refuge in a cave. It was so cold that the ground was covered with frost. A little spider recognized Jesus and wished so much that he could do something to keep Him warm that he spun his web across the entrance of the cave so thick that it hung like a curtain and the cave became warm and cozy.[4]

Another legend imagines that when they arrived at a grove of fruit trees, Jesus commanded the trees to bend down so that Joseph could pluck the fruit; and then Jesus ordered a spring of water to gush from the roots of the tree to quench their thirst. Mary was able to sleep as an angel played a hymn for her on the violin. Wherever they traveled, animals would bow and pay homage to them, and idols would crumble to dust whenever they passed them.

These fictional tales picture something more like a triumphal entry or a holiday trip with fruit, water, nice animals, and symphonic music to soothe their weary minds. And maybe that's what we would expect.

Another legend tells of Mary washing the swaddling clothes of the baby Jesus in their Egyptian home and hanging them on a line to dry. A demon-possessed boy came by and touched some of the clothes, and the demon instantly left him.

Several accounts speak of Jesus' bathwater being especially powerful. It healed a princess of leprosy and anybody else who came into contact with it.

According to the legends and the apocryphal writings, Egypt was a *vacation*. The family's every need was instantly met, and suffering and hardship were eliminated, not only in their lives but also in the lives of everyone around them as little Jesus performed miracle after miracle.

However, we're clearly told in John 2:11 that the turning of water into wine at the wedding feast was the *first* miracle Jesus performed—*the first attesting sign of His deity*—the *arche semeion*.[5] This was the beginning of His miracles, displayed in Cana of Galilee, at the beginning of His public ministry at about the age of thirty. It was not a continuation of miracles that began in childhood.

There were no special miracles to turn Egypt into paradise. There were no angels playing violins or camels bowing to them along the way. The escape of Joseph and Mary and their Child from Bethlehem that night was not aided by miraculously provided food and water. Their long journey to Egypt was the same kind of journey every other ordinary family would have had to endure.

In fact, their journey was *more* difficult than most, for this family was Israel's most wanted. We can easily picture Joseph constantly looking over his shoulder, imagining the clattering of hooves behind every hilltop, wanting to stop and rest longer than they dared.

And all the way to Egypt they must have been asking, "Why?"

What they didn't know at the time was that their going into Egypt and one day returning to their homeland would fulfill Old Testament prophecy. As such, it would help validate the authenticity of the Messiah's claims made approximately three decades later.

We're given a peek here behind the curtain at the sovereign control of God. The evil, cruel paranoia of Herod in attempting to kill Christ was actually used to fulfill the predictions of God's Word and the purposes of God's will. God the Father had said He would call His Son out of Egypt (Hosea 11:1), and now Egypt became His Son's hiding place until Herod died.

In the Old Testament, Israel is often referred to as the son or sons of God. Hosea 11:1 recalls God's calling Israel out of Egypt under the leadership of Moses. Matthew sees God's son, Israel, being brought out of Egypt as pointing forward to *the* Son of God being called out of Egypt. Jesus thus fulfills the type in Hosea's prophecy.

In light of this, it is also interesting to compare Jesus, the Deliverer who was called out of Egypt, with Moses, the deliverer who led Israel out of Egypt.

Moses also avoided a death warrant from the king by his parents' quick action. The Egyptian king, Pharaoh, had ordered the killing of all the newborn Jewish males, but Moses was hidden away and survived and eventually led the people out of bondage.

Hebrews 3:3, however, indicates our Deliverer, Jesus, is *greater* than Moses. Both Moses and Jesus came out of Egypt, and they both led their people out of bondage. But the deliverance of Moses was temporary and insufficient. The deliverance of Jesus Christ is eternal and all-sufficient.

BLOODBATH IN BETHLEHEM

Then when Herod saw that he had been tricked by the magi, he became very enraged, and sent and slew all the male children who were in Bethlehem and all its vicinity, from two years old and under, according to the time which he had determined from the magi. Then what had been spoken through Jeremiah the prophet was fulfilled: A VOICE WAS HEARD IN RAMAH, WEEPING AND GREAT MOURNING, RACHEL WEEPING FOR HER CHILDREM; AND SHE REFUSED TO BE COMFORTED, BECAUSE THEY WERE NO MORE. (Matthew 2:16-18)

Once Herod realized the magi had tricked him and traveled back home by some other route, he was enraged. He would only assume that they had warned the parents of Jesus as well.[6] Thus, he acted quickly—and tragically fulfilled another prophecy.

The actions of Herod literally defy imagination. He was around seventy years of age at this point, diseased, crippled, infected with untreatable venereal diseases so that his intestines were literally rotting; his body guards had to rotate frequently because they could not bear the stench emanating from the pores of his skin. His physicians couldn't heal him; the warm baths couldn't soothe him; his body was covered with ulcers, and his legs were too swollen for him to walk. But no king would have his throne!

Even though he knew his death was imminent, he clutched his throne. He is the perfect picture of depraved, stubborn mankind.

As mentioned earlier, one of his final orders was to round up hundreds of prominent Jewish citizens and incarcerate them inside the arena. He ordered his troops to kill these Jews on the day he died. His command has survived the centuries: "When I die, the Jews may not mourn me, but by the gods they will mourn."[7]

Tragically, instead of the religious leaders, priests, scribes, and rabbis, rushing to Bethlehem to crown the young Messiah as their King, the soldiers of Herod stampeded into town and ripped little boys from their mothers' arms and put them to death. Historical demographers estimate that there could have been thirty or more children under the age of two in Bethlehem and the surrounding area at the time of this rampage.

Matthew connects this event with Rachel's weeping for her children in Jeremiah 31:15. This represented all Jewish mothers who wept over Israel's great tragedy at the time of the captivity. This text in Matthew tells us their weeping was a foreshadowing of the mothers in Bethlehem, who would weep bitterly over the massacre of their little boys.[8]

What makes Herod's crime even more wicked is that he knew the Child he was trying to kill was the Messiah. This first-century antichrist was a pawn in the hands of Satan in attempting to destroy the Seed of the woman, the virgin-born Messiah.

It was Herod who soon died, however, not the young Messiah. Upon Herod's death, his sister and her husband, who were supposed to signal the soldiers to murder the Jews in the arena, instead opened the doors and set the Jewish captives free.

Likewise, when the *final* Antichrist is destroyed, the Jewish nation also will be set free.

NOBODIES IN NAZARETH

But when Herod died, behold, an angel of the Lord appeared in a dream to Joseph in Egypt, and said, "Get up, take the Child and His mother, and go into the land of Israel; for those who sought the Child's life are dead." So Joseph got up, took the Child and His mother, and came into the land of Israel. But when he heard that Archelaus was reigning over Judea in place of his father Herod, he was afraid to go there. Then after being warned by God

in a dream, he left for the regions of Galilee, and came and lived in a city called Nazareth. This was to fulfill what was spoken through the prophets: "He shall be called a Nazarene." (Matthew 2:19-23)

We have seen how the escape into Egypt fulfilled the prophecy of Hosea 11:1 and the massacre in Bethlehem fulfilled Jeremiah's prophecy. There was one more prophecy to be fulfilled in these days of Christ's childhood.

That prophecy is found in verse 23 and concerns where the family resettled in Israel.

After Herod's death, an angel appeared to Joseph in a dream and said, **"Get up, take the Child and His mother, and go into the land of Israel."**

This sounds amazingly familiar, doesn't it? The wording is almost identical to the command to flee into Egypt in verse 13.

The difference is the lack of urgency in verse 20. There's no need to flee, run, hide, or fear. Notice the angel's reassuring message: **For those who sought the Child's life are dead.** Their months of hiding in Egypt were over.

Jesus is still called a *paidion,* so we know he was still a little boy when Joseph and his family embarked on their return to Israel. The text implies that while they were on their way, Joseph learned that Herod's son Archelaus was now ruling over Judea. Archelaus was more wicked than his father! In fact, he inaugurated his reign by killing three thousand Jews in the temple when he suspected an uprising. His reign was so treacherous that even Augustus, the Roman emperor, and no saint himself, finally banished him after nine years of atrocities.

Joseph had every reason to be afraid, and his fears were affirmed when God came to him in a dream and evidently directed him to settle in the village of Nazareth.

Verse 23 tells us this fulfilled **what was spoken through the prophets: "He shall be called a Nazarene."** This seems to be a reference not to a single prophecy but to the general Old Testament prophetic picture of the Messiah being of humble origins and despised.

Nazareth was located about fifty-five miles north of Jerusalem. The inhabitants of the region of Galilee were known for being rough, uneducated, and even uncivilized. Nazareth was an insignificant village—just a common place filled with common, ordinary people trying to make a living. When first told about Jesus years later, Nathanael wondered if "any good thing [could] come out of Nazareth" (John 1:46).

The earthly origins of Christ were as challenging and difficult as one can imagine: an outdoor shelter for a birthplace, on the run as fugitives, immigrating to Egypt and then back to Israel to live in obscurity in a despised village.

Jesus Christ is indeed one of *us*. He is fully God but also fully man. And in many ways, He is far more ordinary than many of us could ever imagine.

And what about the character, obedience and perseverance demonstrated by Joseph and Mary? Their circumstances brought confusion and fear, yet they clung to brief announcements without most of the details and moved from place to place to place in accordance with the divine instructions they were given.

We can draw three important truths from these verses:

- The will of God does not circumvent the challenges of life.

- The love of God does not eliminate attacks by the enemy.

- The promises of God do not lessen the responsibility of the believer.

How easy it is to think that the will of God and the love of God and the promises of God could never mean blood, toil, tears, or sweat. Surely the godly life brings us the good life—ease and freedom from conflict and suffering.

This passage tells us something very different. The beloved Son, His God-chosen mother, and His God-appointed stepfather were fully in God's will and enveloped by God's love. They were used in fulfilling the prophecies of old and God's promises to the world! And what did they encounter? Blood, toil, tears, and sweat.

One author recounted that as he traveled in England, he saw in a graveyard the tombstone of a Cavalier who had lost his property and then his life in battle defending King Charles. The epitaph read: "He served King Charles with a constant, dangerous and expensive loyalty."[9]

What a great testimony it is when we allow the shadow of the cross to fall across our path. It may require blood, toil, tears, and sweat, but it is our privilege to serve our King with a constant, dangerous, and expensive loyalty.

Chapter 10

More Than the Legend of Zeus

Galatians 4:4a

When the queen of England is present at one of her royal residences, her standard is flown from the building. If you see this flag flying somewhere high above the palace, it signifies that the queen is in, the queen has arrived!

This Christmas the world once again will be reminded that the King of the universe has arrived. And for those of us who believe in Him, we have His flag flying from the castle of our hearts.

It is a flag of redemption, for our King came as our Redeemer to die in our place and for our sin.

THE MYSTERY OF CHRIST'S DEITY AND HUMANITY

What an incredible mystery this is! God the Redeemer came to earth as a man—born of a virgin. God chose to dress in the street clothes of our flesh. The eternal second person of the Trinity was confined in time. The omnipresent Son was bound in a Spirit-fertilized egg in a virgin's womb.

We can sing about it and read about and study it, but we can never truly fathom how God did it—how He took on flesh in a virgin's womb. To put it bluntly, none of us has a clue how God could become a baby.

And yet our gospel depends on it. The fact that Jesus Christ was fully God and born fully human is not an optional belief. It is foundational truth.

ATTACKS ON CHRIST'S DEITY AND HUMANITY

It is little wonder, then, that early in the life of the church, the enemy of the church began to develop false teaching that claimed Jesus was something less than fully God or less than fully human.

Before the death of the apostle John, the last living apostle, heretical attacks were being launched against either the full humanity or the full deity of Jesus Christ. One view, known as Docetism, argued that Christ wasn't really human but only appeared to be in the flesh.

John countered in his second epistle, by writing, "For many deceivers have gone out into the world, those who do not acknowledge Jesus Christ as coming in the flesh. This is the deceiver and the antichrist" (2 John 1:7).

The truth is, if Jesus Christ is not fully man and fully God, we cannot be saved and we have no true Christianity. One author put it this way:

> Apart from Jesus being both fully human and fully divine, there is no gospel. The essence and the power of the gospel is that God became man and that, by being both wholly God and wholly man, He was able to reconcile sinners to God.[1]

Jesus' virgin birth, atoning death, resurrection, ascension, and return all stand together, or they all fall together.

If the New Testament is wrong about Jesus being the divine Son of God, born of a virgin, then what in the New Testament can we trust? If the Gospel writers misrepresented the truth about Christ, what else did they lie about?

The satanic attacks against the person of Christ continued in the early centuries of the church, giving rise to various views that stripped from Christ either His deity or His humanity. *Apollinarianism* taught that Christ was not fully human. *Nestorianism* argued that there were two separate persons inside the body of Jesus. And *Monophysitism* taught that Christ had only one nature, which was a fusion of the divine and human. This heresy taught that Christ was neither wholly God nor wholly human but some mixture of both.[2]

The attacks on Christ's nature have not gone away over the years. In fact, they have only intensified.

One British author thought Jesus would have been horrified to think of a church, let alone individuals, worshipping Him as if He were divine.[3] Another writer presented Jesus as a magician who had people under His sway.[4] Still another considered Jesus a great rabbi who had no intention or desire to found a movement or church.[5]

Satan's attacks on the authenticity of Christ's full deity and full humanity have involved more than outright denial of this truth through false teachers. He has also sought to dilute the uniqueness of the virgin birth by counterfeiting it.

Study the religions of the world, and you will be exposed to stories of virgin births. The Romans believed Zeus impregnated Semele without contact with her so that she conceived Dionysus, lord of the earth. Archeologists discovered an ancient Sumerian inscription from long before the birth of Christ that described how their emperor was created in the womb of his mother by their gods. Seven hundred years before the birth of Christ, it was claimed that the goddess of procreation brought about the conception of King Sennacherib in his mother's womb.

Some, of course, conclude from all these virgin-conception stories that Christianity simply borrowed the idea from other religions and came up with its own version.

What they actually reveal is Satan's strategy to predate Christianity with counterfeit versions of the gospel, so that when the gospel event occurred, people could say, "That's nice, but it's old news."

Did Satan really know ahead of time what God had in mind regarding a virgin-born Messiah? Yes! In Genesis 3:15 God told Satan, the "seed" of the woman would crush his head.

Every other time the Bible speaks about human "seed"— literally sperm, or offspring—it's in reference to the seed of man. But in Genesis 3:15 we find the only reference in the Bible to *the seed of the woman.*

Why is this terminology used? Because a woman would conceive without a man, and her offspring, who would be uniquely independent of the seed of man, would crush the serpent. This is a reference to the virgin-born Messiah defeating Satan.

Another text Satan would have access to some seven centuries before the birth of Christ was Isaiah 7:14: "Behold, a virgin will be with child and bear a son, and she will call His name Immanuel."

Satan knew about all this, but instead of surrendering to God's plan, he encouraged and facilitated the development of pagan thought to incorporate the idea of virgin birth.

As a result, the mother of Buddha was said to have seen a great white elephant enter her belly so that she conceived and gave birth to her son. Hinduism teaches that after reincarnations as a fish, tortoise, boar, and lion, the god Vishnu eventually descended into the womb of a woman and was born as her son Krishna. There was even a legend that Alexander the Great was virgin born by the power of Zeus through a snake that impregnated his mother, Olympias.[6]

So, when the Bible says Christ was born of a virgin, the world finds it easy to dismiss, saying, "We've heard that before. Christianity just has its own version of a virgin-born-son myth."

Your philosophy professor in college might tell you that's what happened. Tragically, if he persists in believing that, he will go to hell. Then again, he is depending on hell being a myth too.

Clearly, Satan has spent a lot of energy, passion, time, and effort to deny, attack, dilute, and counterfeit the message of God's Son, the virgin-born Messiah. By Jesus' time his work extended to the point that people had grown accustomed to referring to Herod by the title "King of the Jews." And Caesar Augustus had already taken the title "Savior of the World." So, when the angel appeared to the shepherds and announced, "Today in the city of David there has been born for you a Savior, who is Christ the Lord" (Luke 2:11), they could have said, "We've heard that before." Thankfully, they didn't respond that way.

In pagan religions predating Jesus Christ, initiates were said to be "born again." After going through initiating rights that involved being sprinkled with blood, they were considered born again to a new life. They were even handed a cup of milk to drink, symbolizing they were newborn babes.

Satan has devised counterfeits for many of the great truths of Christianity, such as the virgin birth, the resurrection, and the new birth. Jesus Christ and His church did not borrow these ideas. Rather, Satan had already been at work developing counterfeits that would encourage people to dismiss the claims of Christ as mere legends.

The virgin birth of Christ was one of the key doctrines Satan sought to undermine. Why? Because he knows, better than most, that without the virgin birth—and a Messiah who is fully God and fully man—the world is without a Savior.

Talk-show host Larry King was asked, "If you could select any one person across all of history to interview, who would it be?" Mr. King answered that he would like to interview Jesus Christ. When the questioner followed with, "And what would you like to ask him?" King replied, "I would like to ask him if he was indeed virgin-born. The answer to that question would define history for me."[7]

If the story of Christ's virgin birth is just another legend, just another story, then so is the rest of what the Bible tells us about Him. You can just write it all off. But if it's true, it does indeed *define history for us all.*

One of the most important verses in the New Testament about Christ is one of the first verses in His earthly biography. Matthew 1:18 says it simply enough: "Now the birth of Jesus Christ was as follows: when His mother Mary had been betrothed to Joseph, before they came together she was found to be with child by the Holy Spirit."

It's a simple statement but a great mystery!

In Luke's account, the angel Gabriel explained to young Mary how it would happen:

> "Behold, you will conceive in your womb, and bear a son, and you shall name Him Jesus . . ." Mary said to the angel, "How can this be, since I am a virgin?" The angel answered and said to her, "The Holy Spirit will come upon you, and the power of the Most High will overshadow you." (Luke 1:31, 34-35)

This explains that God the Holy Spirit accomplished it, but do we understand how God can fertilize an egg in a virgin?

I understand it no more than I can understand how God's Son could die for sins I have not yet committed and even now can view me as seated in the heavenlies. I understand it no more than I can grasp how He will one day bring the dust of my buried body back together again in the coming physical resurrection. I understand it no more than I can imagine my glorified and eternal body remaining with Christ in a newly constructed celestial city of gold and pearl, enjoying heaven forever and ever and ever and ever.

We can't fully understand it, but we can confidently affirm what the Bible teaches: Jesus is truly and fully God the Son. He is also fully human. He wasn't just *pretending* to be human: **When the fullness of the time came, God sent forth His Son, born of a woman** (Galatians 4:4a).

NECESSITY OF CHRIST'S DEITY AND HUMANITY

Why Jesus Christ Must Be Fully Human

There are at least three reasons why Jesus had to be fully human.[8]

First, He had to be fully human so that He would, in fact, *be a representative of the human race in His obedience.* The Redeemer had to be a man. The Bible says this:

> As through one transgression there resulted condemnation to all men, even so through one act of righteousness there resulted justification of life to all men. For as through the one man's disobedience the many were made sinners, even so through the obedience of the One the many will be made righteous. (Romans 5:18-19)

Jesus was fully human because He had a human parent. From Mary He received His human nature so that He was truly a member of Adam's race. But while Jesus received from Mary His human nature, He did not have a human father and therefore did not receive a sin nature—what orthodox theologians call inherited guilt—which comes through Adam's sin.

The only way Jesus could be fully human and yet not corrupted with the legal and moral guilt of Adam was to be born apart from the seed of Adam. And there's only one way that could happen: He had to be born *without* the involvement of Adam's seed; He had to be born of a virgin.

Second, Jesus had to be a man so that He could *be a substitute for the human race in His sacrifice.* If Jesus had not been a man, He could not have died in our place and paid the penalty that was due the human race.

God the Son can't die. But God the Son of Man could. Having taken a physical body, the eternal Son of God could experience a physical death. The writer of Hebrews said it this way: "He had to be made like His brethren in all things, so that He might . . . make propitiation [an atoning sacrifice] for the sins of the people" (Hebrews 2:17).

Third, Jesus had to be a man so that He could *experience the penalty of the human race with his death.*

Paul wrote to the Philippian believers, "[Christ was] made in the likeness of men. Being found in appearance as a man, He humbled Himself by becoming obedient to the point of death, even death on a cross" (Philippians 2:7-8).

Jesus Christ faced the wrath of God by becoming sin for us (2 Corinthians 5:21).

Why Jesus Christ Must Be Fully God

While Jesus Christ had to be fully human, there is no salvation in His *birth* or in His *sinless life*. His *teaching* and his *miracles* could not save us.

141

There was a price to be paid for our sins, and someone had to die for those sins and then rise victoriously from the dead. Jesus Christ was born so that He could die and then come back to glorified, resurrected life.

Ah, but in that case, Jesus had to be *more* than fully human. He also had to be fully God. Only one who is fully God could fully bear the penalty for *all* the sins of the world.

John wrote that Christ is "the propitiation [satisfaction] for our sins; and not for ours only, but also for those of the whole world" (1 John 2:2). How does one bear the sins of the whole world?

Let's assume you are a very good person and you sin only three times a day. That's great, but that's still a thousand sins a year.

Now multiply 1,000 by your age. You might even subtract two or three years for the time before you consciously began to sin. If you're an adult, you're still looking at tens of thousands of sins. But you may have to increase your estimate if you consider that every unkind thought, selfish act, lustful idea, covetous thought, or failure to do what you should have done is also a sin. How could you possibly atone for all your sins and the fact that you are sinful?

Here's the truth: We cannot atone for a single sin, let alone the thousands upon thousands we have committed in our lifetime. Much less can we atone for the sins and sinfulness of everybody in our neighborhood or country—or the whole world!

Only God could pay that penalty. And that's precisely the point! God the Son *did* pay the penalty for sin.

*****

The Bible makes it clear:

- It pleased the Lord to bruise Him [the Son]. (Isaiah 53:10 KJV)

- The Lord has caused the iniquity of us all to fall on Him. (Isaiah 53:6)

- He was pierced through for our transgressions, He was crushed for our iniquities. (Isaiah 53:5)

- He Himself bore our sins in His body on the cross. (1 Peter 2:24)

- The wages of sin is death, but the free gift of God is eternal life in Christ Jesus our Lord. (Romans 6:23)

Who is Jesus Christ to you? Is He a baby in a manger? A seasonal interruption? A warm feeling of temporary sanctification? A nice man who was treated cruelly when He didn't deserve it? Is He just one more tradition of religion, another virgin story borrowed from the legends of the world?

Is that what you think? *But what if you're wrong and the Bible is right?*

What if the Bible is telling the genuine virgin-birth story?

If it is, then Christ is more than a myth . . . more than just a baby . . . He is fully God and fully man.

143

Who is Jesus Christ? According to the record of Scripture, Jesus Christ is fully human and fully God.

Since He is both fully God *and* fully man, He is

> fully able to die,
>> fully able to redeem,
>>> fully able to forgive, and
>>>> fully able one day to return!

I invite you to trust the record of Scripture today and receive this virgin-born Redeemer into your life as Savior and Lord.

It will make the singing of Christmas carols much more meaningful. But more importantly, it will prepare you for heaven, where you will sing of this original Christmas Carol—of Christ—forever and ever, without end!

Endnotes

CHAPTER 1

[1] Sue Shellenbarger, "When a Genealogy Hobby Digs Up Unwanted Secrets," *The Wall Street Journal*, January 15, 2013.

[2] Ibid.

[3] Ibid.

[4] Ibid.

[5] Ibid.

[6] Ibid.

[7] "A Long Line of Grandfathers," *Preaching Today*, quoting Linda Click. Preachingtoday.com.

[8] Flavius Josephus, Antiquities of the Jews 20.5.1; cf. Acts 5.36.

[9] Quoted in Daniel Doriani, *Matthew: Volume 1* (P & R Publishing, 2008), 10.

[10] Matthew Henry, *Matthew Henry's Commentary* (Revell, 1900), 5:3.

[11] Douglas Sean O'Donnell, *Matthew* (Crossway, 2013), 33.

[12] Ibid.

[13] John Phillips, *Exploring the Gospel of Matthew* (Loizeaux, 1999), 31.

[14] Ibid.

[15] O'Donnell, 37.

CHAPTER 2

[1] The Vietnam Veterans Memorial, The Wall-USA, thewall-usa.com

[2] Myron S. Augsburger, *The Preacher's Commentary: Matthew* (Word Books, 1982), xi.

[3] William Cowper, "God Moves in a Mysterious Way."

[4] Grant R. Osborne, *Matthew: Zondervan Exegetical Commentary on the New Testament* (Zondervan, 2010), 67.

[5] William Hendriksen, *New Testament Commentary: Matthew* (Baker Book House, 1973), 115.

[6] Osborne, 69.

[7] Ibid., 66.

[8] Ibid.

CHAPTER 3

[1] R. Kent Hughes, *Luke: That You May Know the Truth*, vol. 1 (Crossway, 1998), 30.

[2] Ibid., 31–32.

[3] Warren W. Wiersbe, *Be Compassionate* (David C. Cook, 1998), 23.

[4] Buddy Greene and Mark Lowry, "Mary, Did You Know?"

CHAPTER 4

[1] John MacArthur, *Matthew* (Moody, 1985), 16.

[2] Ivor Powell, *Matthew's Majestic Gospel* (Kregel, 1986), 26.

[3] R. C. H. Lenski, *The Interpretation of Matthew's Gospel* (Augsburg, 1943), 42.

[4] The authors of this ad actually understated the time. According to biblical chronology, Micah's prophecy was about seven hundred years before Christ's birth.

CHAPTER 5

[1] Michael Grant, *The Twelve Caesars* (Charles Scribner's Sons, 1975), 54-55.

[2] Max Lucado, *God Came Near* (Multnomah, 2004), 4.

[3] Philip Yancey, *The Jesus I Never Knew* (Zondervan, 1995), 36-37.

CHAPTER 7

[1] Taken from M. R. James, *The Apocryphal New Testament: Translation and Notes* (Clarendon, 1924).

[2] J. Dwight Pentecost, *The Words and Works of Jesus Christ* (Zondervan, 1981), 62.

[3] G. Campbell Morgan, *The Gospel According to Luke* (Revell, 1931), 40.

[4] John MacArthur, "Testifying to Jesus: Joseph and Mary," sermon manuscript, September 26, 1999. www.gty.org/Resources/Sermons/42-28

[5] William Barclay, *The Gospel of Luke* (Westminster, 1975), 24.

[6] Pentecost, 65.

[7] J. Reiling and J. L. Swellengrebel, *A Translator's Handbook on the Gospel of Luke* (United Bible Societies, 1971), 128.

[8] John Phillips, *Exploring the Gospel of Luke* (Kregel, 2005), 78.

[9] Phil Cross, "Hope Has Hands." Copyright © 2001 Bridge Building Music (BMI) (adm. at CapitolCMGPublishing.com). All rights reserved. Used by permission.

CHAPTER 8

[1] John MacArthur, *God with Us* (Zondervan, 1989), 25.

[2] John MacArthur, *Matthew 1–7* (Moody, 1985), 27.

[3] Ivor Powell, *Matthew's Majestic Gospel* (Kregel, 198), 35.

[4] Stuart Weber, *The Holman New Testament Commentary: Matthew* (Broadman, 2000), 20.

[5] MacArthur, *God with Us*, 71.

[6] James Montgomery Boice, *The Gospel of Matthew, Volume 1: The King and His Kingdom, Matthew 1–17* (Baker, 2001), 31.

[7] Powell, 42.

CHAPTER 9

[1] James Montgomery Boice, *Nehemiah: Learning to Lead* (Revell, 1990), 52.

[2] Fritz Rienecker and Cleon Rogers, *Linguistic Key to the Greek New Testament* (Regency, 1976), 4.

[3] John MacArthur, *Matthew 1–7* (Moody, 1985), 49.

[4] William Barclay, *The Gospel of Matthew,* Volume 1 (Westminster, 1975), 35.

[5] Rienecker and Rogers, 222.

[6] R. C. H. Lenski, *The Interpretation of Matthew's Gospel* (Augsburg, 1964), 80.

[7] John Phillips, *Exploring the Gospel of Matthew* (Kregel, 1999), 46.

[8] MacArthur, 45.

[9] Bruce Larson, *The Communicator's Commentary: Luke* (Word, 1983), 59.

CHAPTER 10

[1] John MacArthur, *Matthew 1–7* (Moody, 1985), 13.

[2] Wayne Grudem, *Systematic Theology* (Zondervan, 1994), 554.

[3] A. N. Wilson, *Jesus: A Life* (Ballentine, 1992).

[4] Morton Smith, *Jesus the Magician* (Hampton Roads Press, 2014).

[5] Geza Vermes, *The Religion of Jesus the Jew* (Augsburg Fortress, 1993).

[6] MacArthur, 12.

[7] Cited by Ravi Zacharias, "Questions I Would Like to Ask God," *Just Thinking*, Winter 1998.

[8] Grudem, 540.